P9-DXO-436

on rice

60 fast and easy toppings that make the meal

by rick rodgers

photographs by frankie frankeny

CHRONICLE BOOKS

SAN FRANCISCO

Text copyright © 1997 by Rick Rodgers

Photographs copyright © 1997 by Frankie Frankeny

All rights reserved. No part of this book
may be reproduced in any form without
written permission from the publisher.

Library of Congress Cataloging-in-Publication Data:

Rodgers, Rick.
        On rice: 60 fast and easy toppings that make the meal / by
Rick Rodgers; photographs by Frankie Frankeny
            p.   cm.
        Includes index.
        ISBN 0-8118-1352-5
        1. Cookery (Rice) 2. Sauces. 3. Quick and easy cookery.
I. Title.
TX809.R5R63 1997
641.6'318—dc20   96-7069
                          CIP

Designed by Melissa Passehl Design

Printed in Hong Kong

Distributed in Canada by:
Raincoast Books
8680 Cambie Street
Vancouver, B.C. V6P 6M9

10 9 8 7 6 5 4 3 2 1

Chronicle Books
85 Second Street
San Francisco, CA
94105

Web Site: www.chronbooks.com

acknowledgments

Writing a cookbook is a team effort, and I am thankful for the key members who played along with me. Bill LeBlond was the first to point out that there was a cookbook in my way of using rice as a main course. Leslie Jonath is a helpful, understanding editor, a soothing hand-holder and resourceful sounding board. Susan Derecskey made the book better with her dedicated attention to detail. Mitzi Dewolfe and Debbie Kibbe of the USA Rice Council were there to supply information about all aspects of the rice industry. And my gratitude to three people who contributed their considerable talents to this book's visual appeal: designer Melissa Passehl, photographer Frankie Frankeny, and food stylist Traci des Jardins.

Special thanks must go out to three people. Diane Kniss is more than just a friend—she is the main reason I ever get any of my recipes onto paper (or disk). With her by my side, chopping, cleaning, shopping, and dishing, the hard work that goes into a cookbook becomes fun. My longtime friend and agent, Susan Ginsburg, kindly gives me personal and professional advice that can only come after knowing someone for years. It is a strange coincidence that Grand Marnier Chocolate Truffles played a large part in my relationships with these very important women in my life. And finally, to Patrick Fisher, who contributes to all of my projects with a hearty appetite, and above all, good humor.

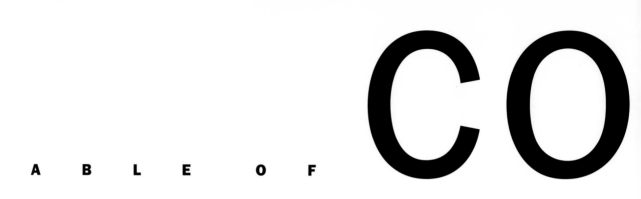

T A B L E O F **CO**

ntents

rice is the staple food for more than one and a half billion people. For more than two thousand years, all over the world, meals have begun with a bowl of rice. In many cuisines, to have a meal without rice is not to have eaten at all.

Although the rice is usually topped by other foods, the meal would not have been as filling without the all-important contribution of rice. Or as tasty—the stir-fries of Asian cooking would seem forlorn unless paired with rice. Nutritious as well, rice is cholesterol-, fat- and sodium-free, easy to digest, perfect for gluten-allergic people, a good source of fiber and vitamins.

American cooks were somewhat slow to appreciate the versatile grain as more than a side dish. We were loathe to give up our typical meal, consisting of a lot of meat and fat and not too much in the way of grains, legumes, vegetables, and fruits. Today's cooks are making up for this oversight with a vengeance, and rice is finally coming into its own.

Sharing in the spotlight with rice is a newfound appreciation for the kind of cooking practiced by the ancient rice-based cuisines. This cooking style features lots of grains, vegetables, fruits, and legumes with moderate amounts of animal-based foods.

Smart cooks have flip-flopped the ingredients of the old-fashioned American meal. In its food pyramid, the U.S. Department

TEOUS rice

of Agriculture (USDA) recommends that grains form the bulk of our diet. Rice is a great way to meet the suggested quota of nine to eleven servings of grains a day. While markets continue to carry the familiar white and brown rice varieties, cooks can also choose from basmati, jasmine, Arborio, Valencia, Asian, and even black rice.

On Rice offers a collection of toppings to spoon over rice or other favorite grains to make a complete main course. This is not the typical rice cookbook. None of the recipes are classic rice pilafs, paellas, or jambalayas—foods cooked with raw rice to make a composite dish. Most are quick-and-easy, hurry-up-and-get-a-fabulous-meal-on-the-table recipes that complement a freshly cooked pot of your favorite rice. The recipes will satisfy both types of cooks—those who like old-fashioned dishes like Chicken Breasts in Jambalaya Sauce (page 63), as well as those who want more exotic, adventuresome fare, such as Brazilian Fish Stew (page 54). For cooks who turn to pasta night after night because of its quick-cooking qualities, rice will provide a change in the bill of fare, and an added advantage. Including the time it takes to boil up a huge pot of water for pasta, rice cooks faster and keeps warm without any loss in quality for a longer period, too. And, with recipes for some rice puddings to round out the menu, *On Rice* brings flavor and convenience to everyday meals.

In China, when friends meet on the street, the greeting translates as "Have you had your rice today?" Even though we're not in Beijing, I hope that *On Rice* gives you many opportunities to answer that question in the affirmative.

Rick Rodgers, May 1996

Asian White Sweet Rice
Brown Sweet Rice

Arborio Italian Rice

Instant Rice
Parboiled or Converted Rice

Short-Grain Brown Rice
Short-Grain White Rice

Medium-Grain Brown Rice
Medium-Grain White Rice

Long-Grain Brown Rice
Long-Grain White Rice

Country Wild Rice Blend

Bhutanese Red Rice
Wehani Rice

Commercial Wild Rice
Hand-Harvested Wild Rice

White Basmati Rice

Black Japonica Rice
Asian Black Rice

Indian Brown Basmati Rice
American Brown Basmati Rice

there are more than 120,000 known rice varieties, and a good number of them have found their way to the marketplace, with more seeming to appear with every trip to the market.

Living in the New York area, I can shop at some of the finest food emporiums in the world, and their shelves are groaning with rice of all sizes, shapes, colors, and price tags. My local supermarket, hardly a gourmet shop, has jumped on the rice bandwagon, too. Rice, formerly restricted to one section where long-grain Carolina reigned, is now discovered all over the store. Japanese sushi rice is found in the Asian department, and others can find their favorite medium-grain rice in the Italian, Latino, or gourmet foods sections.

Clearly, all rice is not the same, and each kind cooks and tastes different. Some are firm, some are soft, some cook into separate grains, and some should be slightly sticky. As a rice lover, you want to be familiar with the three different rice grain sizes, so you can use different rice within each category if you want to substitute or experiment.

Here is a complete rice glossary (even including rice that is not used in this book) to help you sort out the dizzying array of rice available. Basic cooking instructions are found in A Repertory of Rice Recipes (pages 22–29).

grains

White Rice

White rice, also called *polished* or *regular-milled* rice, is the most popular kind of rice. The grain has been hulled, losing vital vitamins and minerals during the milling process. American rice is sprayed with an enrichment coating of B vitamins and soluble iron before packaging. There are three designated lengths of rice: long, medium, and short grain. Each has a different texture after cooking.

Long-grain rice constitutes the bulk of rice sold in American supermarkets. Raw long-grain rice has a long, slender kernel, four times longer than it is wide. When it is properly cooked, the grains are separate, light, and fluffy.

Carolina rice is a familiar brand of long-grain rice but not a particular type. Rice became one of the major crops in the waterlands of North and South Carolina during the American colonial period, but the Civil War effectively destroyed rice as a viable commodity. Today's major rice producing states are Arkansas, California, Louisiana, and Texas.

Asian-style long-grain rice may be found at Asian grocers in large sacks marked with Chinese characters. However, this rice is almost always domestically grown. Both Chinese and Southeast Asians prefer long-grain rice. Carolina rice is very similar and can be substituted.

Aromatic rice is a category of varieties with naturally distinctive scents—they are not artificially scented. The aromas are released as the rice cooks.

Basmati rice, which comes in white, brown, and black colors, is important in Indian cooking; it cooks into firm, separate grains. Its name means "queen of fragrance," to give you an idea of its lovely incenselike bouquet.

Thai jasmine rice has a flowery perfume; it is slightly sticky after cooking.

Domestic aromatic rices include the brand names Texmati and Jasmati. Louisiana produces *wild pecan rice* and *popcorn rice*, which smell very much like the foods in their names but do not necessarily taste like them.

Converted rice is white rice that has been parboiled, then dehydrated. This process ensures separate grains with a firm texture. Converted rice takes a little longer to cook than regular white rice.

Instant rice has been completely cooked, then dried. It can be quickly rehydrated in boiling water; it has very soft grains after cooking.

Boil in the bag rice is the ultimate form of instant rice, very quick and easy indeed. It is up to you to decide if the loss of flavor and texture in these products is worth the convenience.

Medium-grain rice kernels are two to three times longer than they are wide. The cooked grains are moist, tender, and slightly clingy. This stickiness is due to the high amount of the starch amylopectin found in the grains. Many cultures prefer medium-grain rice, including Central American and especially the Caribbean, Italian, and Japanese. In Japan, it is prized because it is easy to pick up with chopsticks. While the Chinese eat long-grain rice with chopsticks as well, their food has thicker sauces than the Japanese; these moisten the rice and help the eater get the food to his or her mouth without dropping it.

Many American cookbooks erroneously refer to some medium-grain rice varieties as short grain. The United States is the only rice-producing country with a separate medium-grain rice category. Other countries generally have only two categories, long (separate, fluffy cooked rice grains) and short (clinging, sticky cooked grains). For example, any reference to Arborio rice as short grain is according to Italian standards; according to the USDA, Arborio is medium grain.

Because of medium-grain rice's starchiness, it is the only rice to use for specialties like risotto and paella—long-grain rice won't work. That starchiness is what makes risotto turn creamy and paella hold together. Even though this book doesn't include the classic versions of those dishes, I still recommend medium-grain rice to add authentic taste. You may use any type of rice you prefer. American medium-grain rice is usually marked on the label in small letters, so look carefully. Look in the ethnic section of the supermarket if it isn't displayed with the long-grain rice, or buy it in a Latino or Asian market.

Italian rice comes in three main varieties, *Arborio*, *Carnaroli*, and *Vialone Nano*. While Italian food experts argue the fine differences among the three, they are virtually interchangeable. Italian medium-grain rice makes the best risotto, although other medium-grain rice can be substituted if absolutely necessary. Some Italians boil their rice like pasta, but the starchiness is reduced by boiling. When boiling rice that will be topped by an Italian sauce, use the inexpensive American medium-grain rice instead of the pricey imported Italian.

Spanish rice is used for the famous Barcelona dish, paella. It is sometimes called paella or Valencia rice. You may substitute any medium-grain rice.

Japanese-style rice, also known as sushi rice, is often misidentified as a short-grain rice. It is rarely imported into this country from Japan, and even if the labeling looks impressively exotic, it was probably produced in California or Texas. It is easily found in Asian groceries or natural food stores. Popular brands include Calrose and its premium brand, Kokuho Rose.

Short-grain rice is almost round, about as wide as it is long. It makes a very sticky rice that is used in certain Asian dishes, mostly desserts. Only a small amount of short-grain rice is sold in this country, most of it as brown rice.

Sweet rice, also known as sticky or glutinous rice, is often used to make Asian stuffings and desserts. Its preparation usually requires an overnight soak and a special steam-cooking process. Some Southeast Asian cuisines use it as a side dish, cooked just like long-grain rice.

Brown, Black, and Wild Rice

Many cooks prefer the pristine white color of hulled rice, but there's much to be said for the texture and flavor of unhulled rices, regardless of their earthy hue. There are three basic kinds: brown, black, and wild.

Brown rice is unhulled rice, which contains the bran, thus retaining more vitamins and fiber. It has a chewy texture and a nutlike flavor. There is generic brown rice and there are brand names of brown rice varieties like Lundberg Farm's *Black Japonica* and *Wehani*. Brown rice comes in long-, medium-, and short-grain varieties, resulting in different levels of stickiness. Brown rice takes longer to cook than white rice (from 45 to 60 minutes). Although brown rice has a slightly higher nutritive value than white rice, the latter is still the sales champion, as illustrated by the millions of Asians who prefer it. This is a cultural matter with roots in Chinese religion. The Chinese believed that hulled rice, being purified of its ugly brown husk, was rendered into a pure white food fit for the gods.

Black rice is brown rice with a dark hull. It is usually available in bulk and rarely labeled by variety, although basmati and jasmine black rice exist. Since it is hard to tell what you are buying, I recommend boiling black rice in salted water until tender (see page 27); it is easier to gauge doneness by this method than by covered cooking.

Red rice is sometimes found in Asian markets. It is usually not cooked as a food but is boiled in water so the resulting red liquid can be used as a food coloring. It is occasionally part of mixed rice blends. (Bhutanese red rice is technically a brown rice and is perfectly edible.)

Mixed rice blends are different types of rice combined for a mixed-hue effect. Follow the cooking directions on the package.

Wild rice is not a rice at all, but a kind of grass. The best wild rice is hand-harvested in small crops from paddies in the north Midwest region. It is also grown as a commercial crop in the Sacramento River delta in California.

other grains: the more, the merrier

Rice is loved around the world and is easy to prepare, but that is not to say it is the only grain worth using as the centerpiece of a meal. In fact, when I was sharing my rice recipes with friends, every now and then someone would exclaim, "This sauce would be fantastic on polenta, too," or "When I make this, I'm going to try it on bulgur," or some other suggestion. It emphasized to me how many Americans have taken all grains to heart.

If you are new to the world of grains, here is a list of some favorite grains. It is admittedly incomplete. More comprehensive information can be found in one of the many grain cookbooks on the market.

Most grains are available in bulk at natural food stores as well as packaged in groceries and supermarkets. While bulk buying reduces the cost, it also means you don't have the advantage of back-of-the-box recipes, which can be frustrating. When in doubt, remember that all grains can be cooked until tender in a large pot of lightly salted water, like pasta. This list gives my preferred cooking method for each grain, with amount needed to yield four to six servings, enough for the topping recipes in this book.

Remember, too, that cooking grains is an inexact science, as their relative age and dryness affect how much water they absorb and how long they take to cook. Cook the grain until it is as tender as you like it, not according to how much water is left in the pot. If the grain is cooked to your liking but there's water left in the pot, drain the grain in a wire sieve.

Amaranth is actually a seed eaten as a grain, considered sacred by the Incas. It cooks into a crunchy porridge with a faintly meaty flavor.

Bring 3 cups of water and ½ teaspoon salt to a boil in a medium saucepan, preferably nonstick, over high heat. Stir in 1½ cups amaranth and reduce the heat to low. Cover and simmer until the liquid is completely absorbed, about 25 minutes. If the amaranth is still soupy, cook, partially covered (so the grain doesn't splatter) over medium heat, stirring often, until the liquid is absorbed.

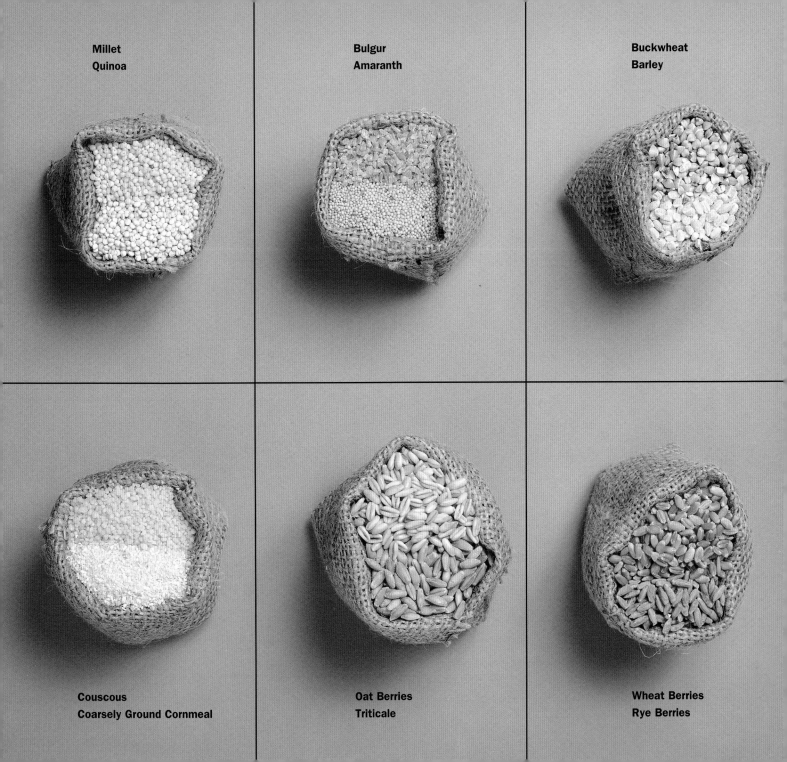

Millet
Quinoa

Bulgur
Amaranth

Buckwheat
Barley

Couscous
Coarsely Ground Cornmeal

Oat Berries
Triticale

Wheat Berries
Rye Berries

Barley is great in a pot of soup but a tasty grain on its own, too. Pearl barley has had the tough outer husk polished off (pearled); this reduces the cooking time. Whole hulled barley has not been polished as completely and needs to be soaked overnight in cold water to cover before cooking. It will take longer than pearl barley and may need more water added if it boils away before the barley is cooked.

Cook 1½ cups pearl barley in a large pot of boiling salted water (or a combination of water and broth) over medium heat until tender, about 45 minutes. Drain well.

Buckwheat groats come packaged plain and roasted. (Groats are grains that have been coarsely crushed; grits are finely crushed.) The coarsely ground roasted buckwheat groats are also called kasha. Kasha requires an unusual procedure to coat the grains before cooking, otherwise they clump together.

In a medium bowl, beat 1 large egg well. Add 1½ cups kasha and stir well to mix. In a medium nonstick skillet over medium heat, cook the egg-coated kasha, stirring gently, until the egg coating sets, about 2 minutes. Transfer to a medium saucepan. Add 3 cups water (or a combination of water and broth), 2 tablespoons unsalted butter, ½ teaspoon salt, and ¼ teaspoon pepper. Bring to a boil over high heat. Reduce the heat to low, cover, and simmer until the liquid is almost completely absorbed, about 15 minutes. Remove from the heat and let stand, tightly covered, until the liquid is absorbed, about 10 minutes.

Bulgur cracked wheat is available in several grinds. Coarse or medium grind is best for main courses.

Bring 3 cups water and ½ teaspoon salt to a boil over high heat in a medium saucepan. Stir in 1½ cups bulgur, return to a boil, and cook for 1 minute. Remove from the heat and cover tightly. Let stand until the bulgur is softened and the liquid is absorbed, about 8 minutes. If necessary, drain the bulgur in a wire sieve and press to extract any excess moisture. Fluff with a fork before serving.

Coarsely ground cornmeal is preferred for making polenta, although it can be made from stoneground fine-grind yellow cornmeal.

Bring 5 cups water (or half milk and half water) and ½ teaspoon salt to a boil in a heavy-bottomed medium saucepan. Gradually whisk in 1½ cups yellow cornmeal. Reduce the heat to medium-low and simmer, whisking constantly, until the polenta is smooth and thick, about 6 minutes. If you like your polenta a bit softer, remove the saucepan from the heat and cover tightly. Let the polenta stand to steam and soften, 5 to 10 minutes.

Couscous is not a grain but small pellets of pasta. I include it here because most people consider it to be and use it like a grain. It comes in semolina and whole wheat varieties, uncooked and precooked, but most of the couscous in this country is precooked or instant. It has become very popular with cooks on the run.

Bring 2½ cups water (or use half broth), 2 tablespoons olive oil, and ½ teaspoon salt to a boil over high heat. Stir in 1⅔ cups instant couscous and remove from the heat. Cover tightly and let stand until the water is absorbed, about 5 minutes. Fluff with a fork before serving.

Millet is best known in the United States as bird seed but becoming popular as a human food, too. It benefits from a light toasting before cooking.

Heat a medium skillet over medium heat. (Have a lid handy, so if the millet pops and jumps as it cooks, the skillet can be covered briefly to contain the seeds.) Add 1¼ cups millet and cook, stirring almost constantly, until the millet is lightly toasted and golden, about 5 minutes. Transfer to a medium saucepan. Add 3¾ cups water (or half water and half broth) and ½ teaspoon salt. Bring to a boil over high heat. Reduce the heat to low, cover tightly, and simmer until the liquid is absorbed and the millet is tender, about 20 minutes. Remove from the heat and let stand, covered, for 10 minutes. Fluff with a fork before serving.

Quinoa is a seed originally from the Andes that is eaten as a grain. It looks slightly translucent when cooked. It should be lightly toasted before simmering.

Heat a medium skillet over medium heat. Add 1½ cups quinoa and cook, stirring almost constantly, until the quinoa is lightly toasted and has turned a slightly darker shade, about 3 minutes. Transfer to a medium saucepan. Add 3 cups water (or half water and half broth) and ½ teaspoon salt. Bring to a boil over high heat. Reduce the heat to low, cover tightly, and simmer until the liquid is absorbed and the quinoa is tender, about 12 minutes.

Rye berries are a favorite grain with Eastern European farmers, as it can grow in colder regions where wheat cannot. The berries have the slightly sour taste that gives distinction to rye bread.

Combine 3 cups water, 1½ cups rye berries, and ½ teaspoon salt in a medium saucepan. Bring to a boil over high heat. Reduce the heat to low, cover, and simmer until the rye berries are tender, about 1 hour. If the berries are not soft enough to your taste, add ½ cup water more and cook for about 10 minutes. To reduce the cooking time by about half, place the rye berries in a large bowl, add enough water to cover by 2 inches, and let stand at room temperature for 8 hours or overnight. (It's convenient to do this in the morning before cooking them for an evening meal.) Drain well before cooking.

Wheat berries are mainly found in health food stores as hard wheat berries. Do not buy small red wheat berries for cooking— they are sold to dedicated bakers for grinding into whole wheat flour in a home grain mill. Wheat berries must be soaked before cooking.

Place 1½ cups wheat berries in a large bowl and add enough cold water to cover by 2 inches. Soak at least 5 hours or overnight. Drain well and place in a medium saucepan. Add 3 cups of water (or half water and half broth) and ½ teaspoon salt. Bring to a boil over high heat. Reduce the heat to low, cover tightly, and simmer until the wheat berries are tender, 50 to 60 minutes. Oat berries, triticale (a hybrid of wheat and rye), *kamut*, and spelt (two ancient types of hard wheat) can be cooked in exactly the same way.

A REPERTORY OF RICE

here are some tips, thoughts, caveats, and recommendations for making failproof rice, followed by a collection of basic recipes, each of which yields about 4½ cups of cooked rice, or about ¾ cup rice per serving, a sufficient amount when served with a stir-fry, sauce, or stew.

Making the Perfect Pot of Rice

Select the right pot: When filled with raw rice and its cooking liquid, the rice cooking pot should not be less than one third nor more than one half full. A heavy-bottomed medium saucepan (two to three quarts) with a tight-fitting lid is ideal for recipes that call for 1½ cups of raw rice. A Flame Tamer is a good precaution against scorched rice.

How much rice to cook: Rice approximately triples in size when cooked. Experienced rice cookers can pour rice into a pot and estimate how much of the pot the rice will fill when cooked. If cooking by the low-tech "knuckle-deep" method (see next page), you can bypass all measuring cups.

Rinsing rice: It is inadvisable to rinse American rice before cooking, because rinsing washes off the nutritive coating

ecipes

that's been sprayed onto the rice. It is also unnecessary since American rice isn't as starchy as that of other countries. Some rice, however, should be rinsed, such as hand-harvested wild rice and imported rice (to remove any impurities) and short-grain sweet rice (to remove excessive starch in an overnight soak). Otherwise, rinsing is mainly a matter of personal taste or cultural background. Some cooks insist that rinsing keeps the grains separate and makes a less sticky pot of rice. In any event, rinsing changes the amount of water needed for cooking since the rice soaks up some of the rinse water. If using rinsed rice, you may need about ¼ cup less liquid than the recipe calls for. Some experts also advise against cooking rice by the boiling method and

rinsing cooked rice (a step that must be done if preparing rice salads). These are not major concerns for Americans who don't center every meal around a bowl of rice as Asians do.

Salting rice: Like all matters of seasoning, how much salt to add to rice is a personal decision. Keep in mind, however, that unsalted rice is very bland. The amount of salt in the recipes can be adjusted as desired.

Low-tech rice cooking: Cooks all over the world use the "knuckle-deep" method for cooking a perfect pot of rice every time. The pot size is very important—when filled with raw rice and liquid, it should be no less than one third full, no more than one half full. Spread the rice evenly in the pot. Add enough cold water to

cover the rice by the depth measured by the first knuckle of your index finger (about ¾ inch). To measure, dip your finger right into the pot until it touches the rice. Add salt to taste. Bring the rice to a boil over high heat and cook for 1 minute. Reduce the heat to low, cover tightly, and simmer, without lifting the lid, until the water is absorbed and the rice is tender, about 12 minutes. Remove from the heat and let stand for 5 to 10 minutes before serving.

High-tech rice cooking: An electric rice cooker is an important appliance in Asian kitchens, since the grain is eaten for breakfast, lunch, and dinner, and so a large pot of cooked rice has to be ready at all times. Unless you eat a lot of rice— and have plenty of counter space—it

may not be practical for your kitchen. If you do purchase a rice steamer, be aware that the instructions may be for Asian medium-grain rice, not the typical American long-grain. Also, Asians habitually rinse their rice before cooking, and Americans don't, which also changes the amount of water needed. The enclosed instructions rarely specify the type of rice, so you should do a test run. If the rice doesn't cook properly, try again, adjusting the water as necessary, using less if the rice was soupy, or more if the rice scorched. For microwave directions, see page 27.

Keeping rice warm: One of the best things about cooked rice is that it keeps warm for up to 30 minutes. Cover the pot tightly, remove from the heat, and let stand in a warm, draftfree place. The texture of rice improves, and it actually tastes better if allowed to stand for 5 to 10 minutes after cooking. This long time period gives the cook a huge window of opportunity to finish cooking the rest of the meal.

Storing rice: White rice will keep almost indefinitely in a dark, dry place, stored in an airtight container. Watch for bug infestation, though, if you anticipate a long storage. Brown rice has oil in the bran layer that can go rancid; store it in the refrigerator for up to 6 months. Leftover cooked rice can be stored, covered, in the refrigerator for up to 3 days. It can also be frozen for up to 2 months.

Reheating rice: For stovetop reheating, place the rice in a heavy-bottomed saucepan. Add 2 tablespoons of water or broth for every cup of refrigerated or frozen rice. Cook over low heat until the rice is heated through, about 5 minutes. For microwave reheating, cover and microwave on High (100%) for 1 minute for every cup of refrigerated rice or 2 minutes for every cup of frozen rice. Let the reheated rice stand, covered, for a couple of minutes before fluffing with a fork and serving. Rice can also be reheated in an electric rice machine, according to the manufacturer's directions.

steamed rice

This is the way most of us were taught to cook rice. Even though fat is included in the recipes on supermarket rice packages, it is totally unnecessary. The cooking times for long-grain rice on the packages may be too long if you prefer firm—not al dente, but firm—rice. For softer rice, use ¼ cup more water and cook for a few extra minutes. For converted, instant, or boil-in-the-bag rice, follow the instructions on the package. This recipe can be adapted to a multitude of variations, which follow.

Makes about 4½ cups

3 cups water (see Note)

1½ cups long- or medium-grain rice

½ teaspoon salt, or to taste

In a heavy-bottomed medium (2½-quart) saucepan, combine the water, rice, and salt. Bring to a boil over high heat. Reduce the heat to low, tightly cover the saucepan, and simmer, without stirring or lifting the lid, until the rice is tender and the liquid absorbed, 12 to 15 minutes. Remove from the heat and let stand for 5 to 10 minutes. The rice will stay hot for up to 30 minutes. Fluff the rice with a fork and serve hot.

Note: For medium-grain rice, use only 2¾ cups water.

Variations

Beef-Flavored Rice: Substitute 3 cups Homemade Beef Broth (page 91) or low-sodium canned beef broth for the water. Add salt to taste.

Chicken-Flavored Rice: Substitute 3 cups Homemade Chicken Broth (page 75) or low-sodium canned broth for the 3 cups water. Add salt to taste.

Fish-Flavored Rice: Substitute 3 cups Homemade Fish Stock (page 55) or 1½ cups bottled clam juice and 1½ cups water for the 3 cups water. Add salt to taste.

Beer Rice: Substitute 1½ cups lager beer and 1½ cups water for the 3 cups water.

Citrus Rice: Stir the grated zest of 1 lemon, lime, or orange into the cooked rice.

Coconut Rice: Substitute 1 cup canned unsweetened coconut milk (page 54) and 2 cups water for the 3 cups water. Stir in 2 tablespoons unsweetened desiccated coconut before cooking.

French Rice: In the saucepan over medium heat, melt 2 tablespoons unsalted butter. Add ½ cup chopped onion and cook until softened, about 3 minutes. Add the rice and cook, stirring often, until it turns chalky white, about 2 minutes. Stir in ½ teaspoon dried thyme. Substitute beef, chicken, or fish broth for the 3 cups water. Add salt to taste.

Herbed Rice: After cooking, stir ⅓ cup chopped fresh basil or ¼ cup chopped fresh dill, cilantro, or parsley into the rice.

Indian Spiced Rice: Substitute basmati rice for the long-grain rice. In the saucepan over medium heat, heat 1 tablespoon vegetable oil. Add 1 teaspoon mustard seeds, 4 cardamom pods, 6 whole cloves, and 1 cinnamon stick. Stir until fragrant, about 20 seconds, then follow the recipe for Steamed Rice. Advise guests to avoid eating the hard whole spices.

Mediterranean Pasta and Rice: In the saucepan over medium heat, melt 2 tablespoons unsalted butter. Add ½ cup chopped onion and cook for 1 minute. Add ½ cup broken dried spaghetti (1-inch pieces) and cook, stirring often, until the spaghetti turns golden brown. Stir in the rice and proceed, substituting beef, chicken, or fish broth for the water.

Saffron Rice: Stir ¼ teaspoon saffron threads, crumbled, into the rice before cooking.

boiled rice

In many parts of Italy, this is the way rice is cooked for everyday meals—just like pasta. Italians would use a local medium-grain rice like Arborio, but the imported rice would be too costly here. Use any long- or medium-grain rice.

Makes about 4½ cups

2 quarts water, broth, or a combination

1½ cups long- or medium-grain rice

2 teaspoons salt

2 teaspoons olive oil (optional)

1. In a large saucepan, bring the water to a boil over high heat. Stir in the rice and salt. Cook, uncovered, without stirring, which could break the rice and release starch, until the rice is tender, about 10 to 12 minutes. Drain well in a wire sieve.

2. To keep the rice warm, toss the cooked rice with the oil. Return to the hot saucepan that the rice was cooked in and cover tightly. The rice will stay warm for up to 10 minutes.

Variation

Boiled Black Rice: Use 1½ cups black rice. Cook just until tender, about 25 minutes. Drain well.

microwaved rice

Cooking rice in the microwave oven doesn't save any time, but it can be handy, as when all the stove burners are full.

Makes about 4½ cups

3 cups water, broth, or a combination

1½ cups long-grain rice

½ teaspoon salt, or to taste

Combine the water, rice, and salt in a microwavesafe 2-quart baking dish. Cover tightly and microwave on High (100%) until the water is boiling, about 5 minutes. Be sure the cooking liquid doesn't boil over. Uncover, being careful of the escaping steam, and stir well. Recover the dish and microwave on Medium (50%) until the rice is tender and the liquid is absorbed, about 15 minutes. Let the rice stand for 5 minutes. It will stay hot for up to 30 minutes. Fluff the rice with a fork and serve hot.

baked rice

Baked rice avoids the problem of scorched rice on the bottom of the pot. The rice also seems to cook up a bit drier and fluffier than with other methods.

Makes about 4½ cups

3 cups water, broth, or a combination

1½ cups long-grain rice

½ teaspoon salt, or to taste

1. Position a rack in the center of the oven and preheat to 350° F.

2. In a 1½-quart flameproof baking dish, combine the water, rice, and salt and cover tightly. Bring to a boil over medium heat. Cover the baking dish tightly.

3. Bake until the rice is tender and the water is absorbed, about 15 minutes. Remove the rice from the oven and let stand for 10 minutes. The rice will stay hot for up to 30 minutes. Fluff the rice with a fork and serve hot.

steamed brown rice

Brown rice has a toothsome flavor and texture, but it is never quick-cooking. Flexibility is the key word when cooking brown rice. It comes in long, medium, and short grain, so be sure to know which kind you have to measure the proper amount of liquid. Don't be frustrated if the rice doesn't absorb all its liquid by the end of the cooking time. Cook it according to desired tenderness, not according to how much liquid is left in the saucepan.

Makes about 4½ cups

3¾ cups water, broth, or a combination (see Note)

1½ cups long-, medium, or short-grain brown rice

½ teaspoon salt, or to taste

In a heavy-bottomed medium (2½-quart) saucepan, combine the water, rice, and salt. Bring to a boil over high heat. Reduce the heat to low, tightly cover the saucepan, and simmer until the rice is tender, 35 minutes to 1 hour, depending on the age and dryness of the rice. If the water cooks away before the rice is tender, add ½ cup of hot water and continue to cook to the desired doneness. Remove from the heat and let stand for 10 minutes. The rice will stay hot for up to 30 minutes. Drain, if necessary. Fluff the rice with a fork and serve hot.

Note: For medium- or short-grain brown rice, use only 3 cups of liquid.

steamed
wild rice

Wild rice, like brown rice, can be temperamental. Depending on many factors, you may have not enough cooking liquid or too much. It is hard to determine just what kind of wild rice you've purchased. Hand-harvested rice is expensive, but one of life's great culinary luxuries. Cultivated wild rice is cheaper and takes less time to cook, but it's pretty darned good, too. Just keep an eye on the level of liquid so it doesn't boil away before the rice is tender. If you like your wild rice firm, cook for the minimum amount of time and expect to drain the rice after cooking. If you prefer puffed, tender grains, cook for the longer period, adding more hot water if needed.

Makes about 4½ cups

1 cup wild rice

3 cups water, broth, or a combination

½ teaspoon salt, or to taste

1. Rinse the wild rice well under cold running water in a wire sieve. Drain well.

2. In a medium saucepan over high heat, bring the water and salt to a boil. Stir in the wild rice. Cover tightly, reduce the heat to low, and simmer until the wild rice is tender, 40 minutes to 1 hour. Let stand for 10 minutes before serving. Drain the wild rice, if necessary. Return to the hot saucepan that the rice was cooked in and cover tightly. The wild rice will stay warm for up to 10 minutes.

how to use the recipes

While there are a few slow-cooked recipes in this book, most of them are what I like to cook after a busy day. I'll put on a pot of rice (the easiest thing in the world), and while it's simmering, cook up a topping to complement whatever rice I've chosen. Some of the recipes can be cooked in under 30 minutes (they are so marked) if you're in a real hurry.

Rice varies in taste and texture, so I've suggested one or two fitting types of rice for each dish, and other grains where appropriate. These are only suggestions. All of the recipes are great with any rice you choose.

Practically all of the recipes make four to six servings and are based on about ¾ of cup rice per person. This should be a sufficient amount for a family of four, as it allows for a couple of extra servings for heartier eaters or for leftovers. If yours is a smaller family, still make the entire topping recipe. Most of these toppings reheat very well for the next day's lunch or dinner, and many freeze well, too.

Many of the toppings are made with meat supplemented by a goodly amount of vegetables and/or beans. The topping works with the rice to create a substantial main course in a bowl or on a plate, depending on how you like to eat your rice. Occasionally you will find a rich dish like the Turkey and Mushrooms in Cream Sauce (page 78), but for everyday cooking, I've tried to keep an eye on fat grams. Meat, poultry, and fish are often used in smaller amounts than usual, more as in the Asian style of cooking. I also recommend non-stick skillets, pots, and woks, which make it possible to cut back on the amount of fat needed to brown meats or soften vegetables.

A large (12-inch) nonstick skillet is used for many of these recipes, especially the ones based on the stir-fry technique. These recipes need a large, shallow pan that will hold all the ingredients; a 12-inch skillet is perfect. Large woks (well-seasoned or nonstick) or flat-bottomed stir-fry pans also work well for some recipes, although you will need to constantly stir-fry the ingredients to be sure they don't burn. If you don't already own a large nonstick skillet, I strongly encourage you to get one. Besides being ideal for these rice toppings, they can be used to sauté an entire cut-up chicken or four large chops, something that usually can't be accomplished without overcrowding in a 9- to 10-inch skillet. If you must make the recipes in a smaller skillet, reduce the recipe by half.

Even though this isn't a conventional rice cookbook, I couldn't resist sharing my four favorite rice pudding recipes. They are all a perfect way to showcase this great grain.

portuguese clams with linguiça

scallops in sherry-garlic sauce

scallops in lemon grass–ginger sauce

shrimp and green beans with peanut sauce

shrimp, fennel, and sun-dried tomato sauté

catfish étouffée

paella sauté with saffron

salmon fillets on broccoli rabe

salmon stroganoff

calamari puttanesca

swordfish in vera cruz sauce

tuna bouillabaisse

sautéed flounder fillets with moroccan pesto sauce

brazilian fish stew

homemade fish stock

FROM THE sea

one

of the best things about cooking fish and shellfish is that they should be cooked quickly to be at their best. When you are pressed for time, they make delicious meals in record time.

Good stock or broth is an essential part of good cooking. Most people use the terms stock and broth interchangeably, although technically a stock is used as an ingredient in a recipe, but a broth is a stock that has been seasoned and is consumed as soup. I have included recipes in this book that create both main courses and chicken, beef, and vegetable broths (see pages 75, 91, and 126). As I have salted the cooking liquid to make the meat and vegetables in the main courses palatable, the resulting liquids are, strictly speaking, broths, not stocks. I also recommend low-sodium canned broths if you're not using homemade.

Fish stock is different—no matter what you do, the cooked fish will be inedible when the broth is strained. Those who like to do things the old-fashioned (and best-tasting way) will find a recipe in this chapter for Homemade Fish Stock (page 55). As a substitute for fish broth, diluted bottled clam juice gives very acceptable results. If you are making a shrimp dish and have the shrimp peels, simmer them in a combination of half clam juice and half water to make a quick shrimp broth. Some fish recipes use chicken broth because the sauce may be too intensely fishy if fish stock is used.

Shellfish-like clams and mussels can be sandy if not handled properly, and there are few things more unappetizing than getting a mouthful of sand in your sauce. Always soak mollusks before using as described on page 36. Make it the first thing you do when preparing a clam or mussel recipe—the mollusks can soak while you chop and measure the other ingredients.

portuguese clams with linguiça

Can Be Cooked in Under 30 Minutes

*Saffron Rice or Steamed Rice
(page 26), preferably made with
medium-grain rice*

36 littleneck clams

3 ounces spicy smoked
   sausage, such as linguiça,
   chorizo, or andouille, cut
   into ¼-inch-thick rounds

1 medium onion, chopped

1 large red bell pepper, seeded
   and chopped

3 garlic cloves, minced

1 cup dry white wine

1 teaspoon dried oregano

¼ teaspoon crushed red pepper
   or freshly ground black pepper

Chopped parsley, for garnish

Lemon wedges, for serving

both of my grandfathers were Portuguese, and the star of every holiday breakfast was a big platter of sautéed linguiça, a garlicky, paprika-scented sausage. I was thrilled to find a thriving Portuguese community in Newark, New Jersey, not far from where I live, and I often visit one of the restaurants in the Ironbound district to get a taste memory of my childhood. This is my standing order—juicy clams spiked with linguiça, cooked in a sauce that was born to be spooned over rice.

1. Scrub and soak the clams as described in the Note.

2. In a dutch oven or flameproof casserole, cook the chorizo with 2 tablespoons of water over medium-high heat, stirring occasionally, until the water evaporates and the chorizo is lightly browned, about 5 minutes. With a slotted spoon, transfer the chorizo to paper towels to drain. Pour off all but 1 tablespoon of the drippings.

3. Add the onion and bell pepper to the dutch oven and reduce the heat to medium. Cook, stirring often, until the vegetables soften, about 5 minutes. Add the garlic and cook for 1 minute. Add the wine, oregano, and crushed red pepper. Bring to a boil over high heat.

4. Add the clams and cover. Cook until the clams have opened, about 5 minutes. Transfer the opened clams to a bowl and cover to keep warm, leaving any unopened clams in the pot. Cover and cook the unopened clams for about 1 minute; if they still don't open, discard them.

5. Spoon the rice into large individual soup bowls, top with the sauce, and sprinkle with parsley. Arrange the clams around the edges of the bowls, and serve immediately with lemon wedges.

Note: To soak mollusks, scrub the clams or mussels well under cold running water. Place in a large bowl and cover with cold water. Stir in ¼ cup cornmeal or flour and let the mollusks stand for about 30 minutes. This helps purge them of their sand, and helps plump them, too. Rinse the clams or mussels well before using. If you have the time, repeat the procedure.

Makes 4 to 6 servings

scallops in sherry-garlic sauce

Can Be Cooked in Under 30 Minutes

Steamed Rice (page 26), preferably made with medium-grain rice

1 tablespoon olive oil

1 large red bell pepper, seeded and chopped

2 ounces thickly sliced prosciutto, finely chopped (½ cup)

6 large garlic cloves, minced

1¼ cups Homemade Chicken Broth (page 75) or low-sodium canned broth

3 tablespoons dry sherry, such as manzanilla

¾ teaspoon sweet Spanish or Hungarian paprika

¼ teaspoon crushed red pepper or freshly ground black pepper

1½ pounds bay scallops

2 teaspoons cornstarch

¼ teaspoon salt

Chopped parsley, for garnish

In Spanish tapas bars, you often find shrimp cooked in a heady garlic sauce. This version uses small bay scallops and a bit of cured ham. If you find only large sea scallops, cut them into ¾-inch cubes. When purchasing the prosciutto, ask for one piece sliced about ¼-inch thick, not the usual paper-thin slices. While it will be more than you need for this recipe, you can freeze the remainder for another use.

1. In a large (12-inch) nonstick skillet, heat the oil over medium-high heat. Add the bell pepper and cook, stirring often, until it begins to brown, about 4 minutes. Add the prosciutto and garlic and reduce the heat to medium-low. Cook until the garlic softens, about 1 minute.

2. Stir in the chicken broth, sherry, paprika, and crushed red pepper and partially cover. Bring to a simmer and cook for 3 minutes. Add the scallops, cover, and cook the scallops for 1 minute.

3. Transfer about ¼ cup of the cooking liquid to a small bowl. Add the cornstarch and whisk to dissolve. Pour into the skillet and cook until the sauce thickens and the scallops are firm and opaque, about 1 minute. Do not overcook the scallops. Season with the salt.

4. Spoon the rice into individual soup bowls and top with the scallops and sauce. Sprinkle with the parsley and serve immediately.

Makes 4 to 6 servings

scallops in lemon grass–ginger sauce

Can Be Cooked in Under 30 Minutes

Steamed Rice (page 26), preferably made with jasmine rice

2 stalks lemon grass (see Note) or grated zest of 1 lime

¾ cup Homemade Chicken Broth (page 75) or low-sodium canned broth

3 tablespoons Asian fish sauce (see Note)

1 tablespoon light brown sugar

1 tablespoon rice vinegar

½ teaspoon crushed red pepper

⅓ cup cornstarch

⅛ teaspoon salt

⅛ teaspoon freshly ground black pepper

1 pound sea scallops

2 tablespoons vegetable oil

¼ cup chopped shallots or scallions, white parts only

1 tablespoon minced fresh ginger

3 medium carrots, cut diagonally into ¼-inch-thick slices

6 large shiitake mushrooms, stems discarded, caps cut into ¼-inch-thick slices

1 can (15 ounces) cut baby corn, drained and rinsed

½ cup canned sliced water chestnuts, drained and rinsed

Cilantro leaves, for garnish

lemon grass, with its refreshing citrus scent and flavor, combines with other Southeast Asian flavors to create a spicy sauce for scallops. Sea scallops work better than bay scallops in this dish. Cut them in half or even quarters if they are very big.

1. Remove the tough outer layer of the lemon grass. Using a sharp knife or a mini-food processor, mince the tender bottom 4 to 6 inches of the stalks. You should have about ¼ cup. Set aside.

2. In a small bowl, mix the chicken broth, fish sauce, brown sugar, rice vinegar, and crushed red pepper. Set aside.

3. In a medium bowl, combine the cornstarch, salt, and pepper. Coat the scallops in the cornstarch, shaking off the excess. Heat a large (12-inch) nonstick skillet over medium-high heat until hot. Add 1 tablespoon of the oil, tilt the skillet to coat the bottom with the oil, and heat until the oil is very hot. Add the scallops and cook, turning once, until lightly browned, about 4 minutes. Transfer to a plate and set aside.

4. Add the remaining 1 tablespoon oil to the skillet and heat. Add the lemon grass, shallots, and ginger. Stir until the shallots are softened, about 1 minute. Add the carrots and mushrooms and stir-fry for 1 minute. Add the baby corn and water chestnuts and stir-fry until the carrots are crisp-tender, about 3 minutes. Add the chicken broth mixture and bring to a boil. Add the scallops, stirring to coat the scallops completely with the sauce, and cook until the sauce is thickened, about 1 minute.

5. Spoon the rice into individual soup bowls and top with the scallops, vegetables, and sauce. Sprinkle each serving with cilantro leaves and serve immediately.

Note: Lemon grass and Asian fish sauce *(nam pla or nuoc mam)* are available in Asian markets, many supermarkets, or by mail order (see page 140). A combination of equal amounts of soy sauce, Worcestershire sauce, and water may be substituted for the fish sauce.

Makes 4 to 6 servings

shrimp and green beans with peanut sauce

Can Be Cooked in Under 30 Minutes

Steamed Rice (page 26), preferably made with long-grain rice

Peanut Sauce

1 tablespoon vegetable oil

½ cup finely chopped shallots or scallions, white parts only

1 tablespoon chopped fresh ginger

2 garlic cloves, minced

2 teaspoons Thai yellow curry paste (see Note) or Madras curry powder

1 cup canned unsweetened coconut milk (see Note) or heavy cream

½ cup Homemade Chicken Broth (page 75) or low-sodium canned broth

½ cup unsalted peanut butter

2 tablespoons Asian fish sauce (see Note)

2 tablespoons fresh lime juice

2 teaspoons brown sugar

Salt

Crushed red pepper

¾ pound green beans, trimmed and cut into ½-inch lengths

Nonstick vegetable oil spray

1½ pounds medium shrimp, peeled and deveined

Chopped cilantro, for garnish

my first job in the New York restaurant world was with a Thai chef on Manhattan's Upper West Side who taught me how to make an authentic peanut sauce. He served it with grilled pork kebabs (satay), but I loved it so much, I would pour it onto rice and top it with other items from the menu like shrimp and green beans.

1. To make the peanut sauce, in a heavy-bottomed medium saucepan, heat the oil over medium heat. Add the shallots, ginger, and garlic. Cook, stirring often, until the shallots soften, about 2 minutes. Add the curry paste and cook, stirring constantly to break up the paste, until fragrant, about 1 minute. Be careful not to scorch the curry paste.

2. Add the coconut milk, chicken broth, peanut butter, fish sauce, lime juice, and brown sugar. Whisking constantly, bring to a simmer. Reduce the heat to low and simmer until slightly thickened, about 5 minutes. Season with salt and crushed red pepper to taste. Keep the sauce warm. If the sauce thickens upon standing, thin with additional chicken broth.

3. In a large (12-inch) nonstick skillet, bring ½ cup lightly salted water to a boil over high heat. Add the green beans and cover. Cook until the beans are crisp-tender, about 3 minutes. Drain and set aside. Wipe the skillet dry.

4. Spray the skillet with the cooking oil spray and heat over medium-high heat. Add the shrimp and cook, stirring often, just until the shrimp turn pink, about 3 minutes. Add the green beans during the last 30 seconds of cooking, just to heat them through.

5. Spoon the rice into individual soup bowls and top with the peanut sauce. Divide the shrimp and green beans among the bowls, sprinkle with cilantro, and serve immediately.

Note: Thai curry paste, unsweetened coconut milk, and fish sauce are available at Asian markets or by mail order (page 140).

Makes 4 to 6 servings

shrimp, fennel, and sun-dried tomato sauté

Can Be Cooked in Under 30 Minutes

French Rice or Steamed Rice (page 26), preferably made with long-grain rice

2 tablespoons olive oil

1 medium onion, chopped

1 medium bulb (14 ounces) fennel, base trimmed and fronds removed, cut into ½-inch dice (about 2½ cups)

1¾ cups Homemade Chicken Broth (page 75) or use low-sodium canned broth

½ cup dry vermouth

4 teaspoons chopped fresh rosemary or 1½ teaspoons dried rosemary

1½ pounds medium shrimp, peeled and deveined

½ cup (2 ounces) coarsely chopped oil-packed sun-dried tomatoes

1 tablespoon unsalted butter, chilled, cut up

¼ teaspoon salt

¼ teaspoon freshly ground black pepper

Chopped fennel fronds, for garnish (optional)

f ennel, sometimes called anise, is a star in the Mediterranean vegetable roster. It is unfairly underappreciated on these shores, perhaps because we associate it with licorice. True, it does have a hint of licorice flavor—more noticeable in the raw bulb or feathery fronds—but it diminishes when cooked, leaving behind a firm celery-like texture.

1. In a large (12-inch) nonstick skillet, heat the oil over medium heat. Add the onion and cover. Cook, stirring often, until the onion is golden, about 6 minutes. Stir in the fennel, cover, and cook until the fennel is crisp-tender, about 5 minutes. Add the broth, vermouth, and rosemary and boil, uncovered, until the liquid reduces slightly, about 3 minutes.

2. Add the shrimp and sun-dried tomatoes and reduce the heat. Cover and cook until the shrimp are pink and firm, about 3 minutes. Remove the skillet from the heat and stir in the butter. Season with the salt and pepper.

3. Spoon the rice into individual serving bowls. Top with the shrimp and fennel, garnish with chopped fronds, if desired, and serve immediately.

Makes 4 to 6 servings

catfish étouffée

Can Be Cooked in Under 30 Minutes

Beer Rice or Steamed Rice (pages 26),
  preferably made with popcorn rice
  or long-grain rice

¼ cup all-purpose flour

1 tablespoon vegetable oil

1 medium onion, chopped

1 celery rib with leaves, chopped

1 small red bell pepper,
  seeded and chopped

2 large garlic cloves, minced

2 cups Homemade Fish Stock
  (page 55) or 1 cup bottled clam
  juice and 1 cup water

1 can (28 ounces) Italian plum
  tomatoes, drained and coarsely
  chopped

2 tablespoons Cajun Seasoning
  (recipe follows)

1 tablespoon Worcestershire sauce

1 bay leaf

1½ pounds catfish fillets,
  cut into strips 2 inches long
  and 1 inch wide

2 scallions, chopped

1 tablespoon unsalted butter, cut up

¼ teaspoon salt

Hot pepper sauce (optional)

Chopped parsley, for garnish

É touffée, as any Cajun can tell you, means "smothered," and it is a favorite way to serve seafood swimming in a spicy sauce. One of its secrets is a long-cooked, browned flour and fat mixture called roux. I endorse the quicker, reduced-fat method popularized by Paul Prudhomme.

1. Heat a large (12-inch) nonstick skillet over medium heat for 2 minutes. Add the flour and stir constantly, shaking the pan often, until the flour turns dark beige, about 5 minutes. Be careful not to let the flour scorch. Immediately transfer the browned flour to a plate and set aside.

2. Heat the oil in the skillet over medium heat. Add the onion, celery, bell pepper, and garlic. Cover and cook until the vegetables soften, about 4 minutes. Add the browned flour and stir well.

3. Add the fish stock, tomatoes, Cajun Seasoning, Worcestershire sauce, and bay leaf and bring to a simmer. Reduce the heat to low, partially cover, and simmer until the sauce reduces slightly, about 10 minutes. Add the catfish and scallions. Cook until the fish is opaque, about 3 minutes. Remove from heat, add the butter, and stir gently until the butter is melted. Season to taste, with the salt and hot pepper sauce, if using. Remove and discard the bay leaf.

4. Spoon the rice into individual soup bowls and top with the étouffée, sprinkling each serving with the parsley.

Variation

Shellfish Étouffée: Substitute 1 pound of either medium shrimp, deveined, crawfish tails, shelled, or crabmeat for the catfish. Cook until the shrimp turns pink and firm or the crawfish or crab is heated through, about 3 minutes.

Cajun Seasoning

Mix 2 tablespoons sweet Hungarian paprika, 1 teaspoon each dried basil and dried thyme, ½ teaspoon each freshly ground black pepper, garlic powder, and onion powder, and ¼ teaspoon ground hot red pepper. Use as an all-purpose savory seasoning in étouffées, fish breading, fried chicken, vegetables, and salad dressings. (Store, tightly covered, in a cool dry place.)

Makes 4 to 6 servings

paella sauté
with saffron

Can Be Cooked in Under 30 Minutes

Chicken-flavored Rice or Steamed Rice (page 26), preferably made with medium-grain rice

3 ounces chorizo or other spicy smoked sausage, such as linguiça or andouille, cut into ¼-inch dice

1½ pounds medium shrimp, peeled and deveined

1 tablespoon olive oil

2 scallions, chopped

1 small red bell pepper, seeded and chopped

2 garlic cloves, minced

½ cup thawed frozen peas

1 teaspoon dried oregano

¼ teaspoon saffron threads, crumbled

1¼ cups Homemade Fish Stock (page 55) or ¾ cup bottled clam juice and ½ cup water

½ cup dry white wine

¼ teaspoon crushed red pepper or freshly ground black pepper

2 teaspoons cornstarch

¼ teaspoon salt

Hot pepper sauce

Chopped parsley, for garnish

Clearly inspired by the vibrant flavors of paella, I have served this to company for casual Saturday-night suppers, and they liked it as much as the far more complicated classic version.

1. In a large (12-inch) nonstick skillet, cook the chorizo with 2 tablespoons of water over medium-high heat, stirring occasionally, until the water evaporates and the chorizo is lightly browned, about 5 minutes. With a slotted spoon, transfer the chorizo to paper towels to drain, leaving the drippings in the skillet.

2. Add the shrimp to the skillet and cook, stirring often, just until pink and firm, 2 to 3 minutes. Set aside with the sausage.

3. Add the oil to the skillet and heat over medium heat. Add the scallions, red pepper, and garlic. Reduce the heat to medium-low and cover. Cook until the vegetables soften, about 4 minutes. Stir in the peas, oregano, and saffron.

4. In a small bowl, combine the fish stock, wine, and crushed red pepper. Whisk in the cornstarch to dissolve. Stir into the skillet and bring to a simmer. Return the shrimp and chorizo to the skillet, and cook until the sauce thickens and the shrimp and chorizo are heated through, about 1 minute. Season with salt and hot pepper sauce to taste.

5. Spoon the rice into individual soup bowls and top with the shrimp, sausage, and sauce. Sprinkle with the parsley and serve immediately.

Variation

Chicken Paella Sauté: Substitute 1½ pounds boneless and skinless chicken breast, cut into strips 2 inches long and ½ inch thick, for the shrimp. Cook in the chorizo drippings in the skillet until lightly browned, about 5 minutes, then set aside with the chorizo. Continue with steps 3, 4, and 5.

Makes 4 to 6 servings

salmon fillets on broccoli rabe

French Rice made with chicken broth or Steamed Rice (page 26), preferably made with long-grain rice

⅓ cup pine nuts

1 tablespoon olive oil

5 anchovy fillets in oil, drained and minced, or 1 tablespoon anchovy paste

3 garlic cloves, minced

¼ teaspoon crushed red pepper or freshly ground black pepper

2 pounds broccoli rabe, well rinsed, stems cut into ½-inch pieces, and the remainder coarsely chopped

¾ cup Homemade Chicken Broth (page 75) or low-sodium canned broth

⅓ cup raisins

½ teaspoon salt

2 pounds salmon fillets, cut into 4 to 6 pieces

⅛ teaspoon freshly ground black pepper

Lemon wedges, for serving

broccoli rabe is no shrinking violet—its imperious flavor must be tempered by long cooking. Sicilians balance its bitterness with the sweet and salty accents of raisins, pine nuts, and anchovies. Salmon matches broccoli rabe strength for strength. Rice pulls all these strong flavors together, making this a great autumn dish for greens lovers.

1. Heat a large (12-inch) nonstick skillet over medium heat. Add the pine nuts and cook, stirring almost constantly, until toasted and golden brown, 2 to 3 minutes. Transfer to a plate and set aside.

2. Add the oil to the skillet and heat. Add the anchovies, garlic, and crushed red pepper. Stir until the garlic is lightly colored, about 1 minute. In batches, add the broccoli rabe, covering and letting the first batch wilt before adding the next batch. Stir in the toasted pine nuts, the chicken broth, raisins, and ¼ teaspoon of the salt. Reduce the heat to low. Simmer, covered, until the broccoli rabe is very tender, about 45 minutes.

3. Season the salmon with the remaining ¼ teaspoon salt and the pepper. Place the fillets on top of the broccoli. Cover and cook until the salmon is barely rosy in the thickest part of the fillet when prodded with the tip of a knife, about 8 minutes.

4. Spoon the rice onto individual dinner plates. Top each serving with the broccoli rabe, and then a salmon fillet. Serve immediately with the lemon wedges.

Makes 4 to 6 servings

salmon stroganoff

Can Be Cooked in Under 30 Minutes

French Rice made with fish stock or Steamed Rice (page 26), preferably made with long-grain rice

¼ cup all-purpose flour

Salt

Freshly ground black pepper

1½ pounds skinless salmon fillets, cut crosswise into strips about ¾ inch wide

2 tablespoons vegetable oil

1 tablespoon unsalted butter

⅓ cup finely chopped shallots or scallions, white parts only

10 ounces mushrooms, sliced

1 tablespoon chopped dill

1 cup Homemade Chicken Broth (page 75) or low-sodium canned broth

½ cup reduced-fat sour cream

Salmon and mushrooms in a dilled sour cream sauce sounds even more Russian than the familiar version with beef. Fresh dill is a must in this recipe. While very good on rice, the stroganoff may be even better over bulgur or kasha.

1. In a medium bowl or plastic bag, combine the flour, ¼ teaspoon salt, and ¼ teaspoon pepper. Toss the salmon strips in the flour, shaking off the excess. In a large (12-inch) nonstick skillet, heat the oil over medium-high heat. Add the salmon to the skillet. Cook until the underside browns lightly, about 2 minutes. Using a wide spatula, carefully turn the salmon strips, avoiding breaking them as much as possible. Continue to cook until the other side browns, about 2 minutes more. Transfer to a plate and set aside.

2. Add the butter to the skillet and melt. Add the shallots and stir until they soften, about 30 seconds. Add the mushrooms and dill. Cook, stirring occasionally, until the mushrooms give off their liquid and brown lightly, about 6 minutes. Stir in the chicken broth.

3. Return the salmon to the skillet and bring to a simmer. Reduce the heat to low and cook for 1 minute. Remove from heat. Stir in the sour cream, again trying not to break up the salmon too much. Return to the heat and cook just until heated through but not boiling. Season with salt and pepper to taste.

4. Spoon the rice into individual soup bowls. Top with the salmon, mushrooms, and sauce, and serve immediately.

Makes 4 to 6 servings

calamari puttanesca

Can Be Cooked in Under 30 Minutes

Boiled Rice (page 27), preferably made with medium-grain rice

1 tablespoon olive oil

1 medium onion, chopped

3 anchovy fillets in oil, rinsed and chopped, or 1 teaspoon anchovy paste

2 garlic cloves, minced

1 can (28 ounces) Italian plum tomatoes in puree, coarsely chopped

½ cup (4 ounces) black Mediterranean olives, pitted

⅓ cup red wine

¼ cup chopped fresh basil or 1½ teaspoons dried oregano

3 tablespoons small capers, rinsed

¼ teaspoon crushed red pepper, or more to taste

1 pound squid, tentacles cut off and coarsely chopped, sacks cut into ¼-inch rings

Salt

my fish purveyor is Italian, and he told me that his family has this dish every Christmas Eve at their traditional all-fish midnight supper, although their batch is about five times the amount of this one. He also gave me this tip: Don't wash off any ink that may be left on the squid, or calamari as he calls it; it will add flavor, body, and a deep color to the sauce. Served on top of a bowl of hot steaming rice, this recipe makes great nonholiday fare, too.

1. In a dutch oven or flameproof casserole, heat the oil over medium heat. Add the onion and cook, stirring often, until golden, about 5 minutes. Add the anchovies and garlic and stir, breaking up the anchovies, for 1 minute.

2. Stir in the tomatoes with their puree, the olives, wine, basil, capers, and crushed red pepper. Bring to a boil. Simmer briskly until slightly reduced, about 5 minutes.

3. Stir in the squid and cook until the squid is just tender and opaque, about 3 minutes. Salt to taste.

4. Spoon the rice into individual soup bowls and top with the squid and sauce. Serve immediately.

Makes 4 to 6 servings

swordfish in vera cruz sauce

Can Be Cooked in Under 30 Minutes

Steamed Rice (page 26), preferably made with long-grain rice

1 tablespoon olive oil

1 medium onion, chopped

2 large garlic cloves, minced

2 cans (16 ounces each) or 1 can (28 ounces) plum tomatoes, juice reserved, coarsely chopped

½ cup small pimiento-stuffed green olives

3 tablespoons fresh lime juice

2 tablespoons capers, rinsed

1 tablespoon chopped pickled jalapeños, or more to taste

1 teaspoon dried oregano

1 teaspoon dried marjoram

1 bay leaf

1½ pounds swordfish steak, ¾ inch thick, skin removed, cut into 1-inch pieces

¼ teaspoon salt

Chopped cilantro, for garnish

Pickled jalapeño peppers, now available in supermarkets thanks to the popularity of nachos, add a particular zip to this sauce that fresh chiles don't offer. If you really like their *picante* kick, you can heat up the sauce even more with a tablespoon or so of the pickle juice. Olives, capers, and lime juice add their assertive flavors to make a tomato sauce to remember. Try it with other firm fish, such as shark or tuna.

1. In a large dutch oven or flameproof casserole, heat the oil over medium heat. Add the onion. Cook, stirring often, until it softens, about 4 minutes. Add the garlic and cook for 1 minute.

2. Add the tomatoes with their juices, olives, lime juice, capers, pickled jalapeños, oregano, marjoram, and bay leaf and bring to a simmer. Reduce the heat to medium-low and simmer, uncovered, stirring often, until the tomato juices thicken, about 15 minutes.

3. Stir in the swordfish cubes and cover. Cook until the swordfish is just firm and opaque, about 4 minutes. Season with the salt. Discard the bay leaf.

4. Spoon the rice into individual soup bowls and top with the swordfish and sauce. Sprinkle with cilantro and serve immediately.

Makes 4 to 6 servings

tuna bouillabaisse

Can Be Cooked in Under 30 Minutes

French Rice, Fish-Flavored Rice, or Steamed Rice (page 26), preferably made with long-grain rice

1 tablespoon olive oil

1 small bulb fennel, base trimmed and fronds removed, chopped into ½-inch pieces (about 1½ cups)

3 medium leeks, white parts only, chopped (about 1 cup)

2 garlic cloves, minced

1 can (28 ounces) Italian plum tomatoes in juice, juices reserved, chopped

1 cup Homemade Fish Stock (page 55) or ½ cup bottled clam juice and ½ cup water

½ cup dry vermouth or white wine

2 teaspoons Herbes de Provence (page 121)

1 strip (4 inches) orange zest removed from the orange with a vegetable peeler

¼ teaspoon saffron, crumbled

¼ teaspoon salt

¼ teaspoon crushed red pepper

1½ pounds tuna steaks, ¾ inch thick, cut into ¾-inch cubes

a true bouillabaisse is made with a large collection of fish and shellfish, but this simplified version is welcome on busy nights when you crave Provençale flavors in short order. Try it with any firm-fleshed fish, like cod, swordfish, or snapper.

1. In a large dutch oven or flameproof casserole, heat the oil over medium heat. Add the fennel and leeks. Cover and cook, stirring often, until the vegetables soften, about 6 minutes. Add the garlic and cook for 1 minute.

2. Stir in the tomatoes with their juices, fish stock, vermouth, Herbes de Provence, and orange zest. Bring to a simmer. Reduce the heat to medium-low. Cook, uncovered, until the liquid is reduced by half, about 20 minutes. During the last 5 minutes, stir in the saffron, salt, and crushed red pepper. Remove the orange zest.

3. Add the tuna and cover. Cook until the tuna is just firm and opaque, about 5 minutes.

4. Spoon the rice into individual soup bowls. Top with tuna and sauce and serve immediately.

Makes 4 to 6 servings

sautéed flounder fillets with moroccan pesto sauce

Can Be Cooked in Under 30 Minutes

Saffron Rice or Steamed Rice (page 26), preferably made with long-grain rice

Charmoula

1 cup cilantro leaves

½ cup parsley leaves

3 tablespoons fresh lemon juice

1 teaspoon sweet Hungarian paprika

2 garlic cloves

¼ teaspoon salt

⅛ teaspoon ground red pepper

½ teaspoon ground coriander

½ teaspoon cumin seeds, toasted
and crushed (see page 124)

¼ teaspoon sweet Hungarian
paprika

½ teaspoon salt

⅛ teaspoon ground hot pepper

1½ pounds flounder fillets,
cut into 4 to 6 pieces

1 tablespoon olive oil

½ cup Homemade Fish Stock
(page 55) or bottled clam juice

Spices and herbs form the backbone of Moroccan cooking. *Charmoula,* a pestolike sauce made with cilantro, parsley, and spices, is served with many North African fish dishes, such as these spice-dusted sautéed flounder fillets. The rice soaks it all up admirably, but this is also great on couscous, too, of course. Since the dish doesn't have any vegetables, serve it with a carrot salad.

1. To make the *charmoula,* in a food processor fitted with the metal blade, pulse all of the ingredients until very finely chopped. Transfer to a bowl and set aside.

2. In a small bowl, combine the coriander, cumin, paprika, salt and ground hot pepper. Season both sides of the flounder fillets with the spice mixture.

3. In a large (12-inch) nonstick skillet, heat the oil over medium-high heat. Add the fish and cook, turning once, until just opaque in the thickest part of the fillet when prodded with the tip of a knife, about 5 minutes. Transfer the fish to a plate and keep warm.

4. Pour the fish stock into the skillet and bring to a boil. Remove from the heat and stir in the *charmoula.*

5. Spoon the rice into individual soup bowls or onto plates. Top each serving with the sauce and a fish fillet. Serve immediately.

Makes 4 to 6 servings

brazilian fish stew

Can Be Cooked in Under 30 Minutes

*Coconut Rice or Steamed Rice
(page 26), preferably made with
medium-grain rice*

2 pounds cod, scrod, or haddock
fillets, cut into 1-inch pieces

3 tablespoons fresh lime juice

1 tablespoon olive oil

1 medium onion, chopped

1 medium green bell pepper,
seeded and chopped

2 large garlic cloves, minced

1 pound ripe plum tomatoes, peeled,
seeded, and chopped (see Notes),
or 1 can (16 ounces) Italian plum
tomatoes, drained and chopped

1 cup Homemade Fish Stock
(page 55) or bottled clam juice

⅔ cup canned unsweetened
coconut milk (see Notes)

¼ cup chopped cilantro

¼ teaspoon salt

¼ teaspoon ground red pepper

big, bold and beautiful, Brazilian cooking has African, Portuguese, and native influences, which result in some wonderfully seasoned dishes. Coconut milk plays a large part in this cuisine. While coconut milk can be freshly made, the cans are a useful pantry item. Be careful not to purchase cream of coconut, which is very sweet and used to make piña coladas and some desserts, not savory dishes. Quinoa makes an interesting substitute for rice for this exotic dish.

1. In a medium bowl, toss the fish and lime juice. Set aside to marinate while preparing the tomato-coconut sauce.

2. In a large (12-inch) nonstick skillet, heat the oil over medium heat. Add the onion, bell pepper, and garlic. Cook, stirring often, until the onion softens, about 5 minutes. Add the tomatoes, stock, coconut milk, and cilantro. Bring to a simmer and reduce the heat to medium-low. Simmer, partially covered, for 10 minutes.

3. Add the fish and the marinating juices. Cook, uncovered, until the fish is firm and opaque, 4 to 5 minutes. Season with the salt and ground red pepper.

4. Spoon the rice into individual soup bowls and top with the stew. Serve immediately.

Notes

Canned unsweetened coconut milk is available at ethnic markets and many supermarkets and by mail order (see page 140).

To peel tomatoes, bring a large saucepan of water to a boil over high heat. A few at a time, drop in the tomatoes and cook until the peels loosen, 30 to 60 seconds. (Ripe tomatoes take the least amount of time.) Using a slotted spoon, transfer the tomatoes to a large bowl of cold water. Repeat with all the tomatoes. Use a small sharp knife to remove the peels. To seed the tomatoes, cut them in half and squeeze gently to remove the seeds (they may need to be prodded out with the tip of a finger).

Variation

Brazilian Fish Stew with Shellfish: Use 1½ pounds cod. After the cod has simmered for 1 minute, add ½ pound medium shrimp, shelled and deveined, or scallops and continue to cook until the fish and shellfish are firm and opaque, about 3 minutes.

Makes 4 to 6 servings

homemade fish stock

2 pounds fish bones, heads, and trimmings, well rinsed and coarsely chopped

1 medium onion, chopped

1 medium carrot, chopped

1 medium celery rib with leaves, chopped

2 quarts water

1 cup dry vermouth or white wine (optional)

4 sprigs of parsley

½ teaspoon dried thyme

1 bay leaf

¼ teaspoon black peppercorns

ask your fish store for bones, heads, and trimmings (gills and viscera removed) of lean-fleshed fish such as cod, flounder, snapper, and porgy, in any combination. Salmon, mackerel, and bluefish are too oily; they make an overly strong stock. Most supermarket fish departments aren't too well supplied with fish trimmings, so use the least expensive bone-in fish available, cut into large chunks. Fish stock is simmered for only 30 minutes, so you will get savory results in short order.

1. Place the fish bones, onion, carrot, and celery in a large pot. Add enough of the water to cover and add the wine, if using. Bring to a simmer over medium-high heat, skimming off any foam that rises to the surface. Add the parsley, thyme, bay leaf, and peppercorns. Reduce the heat to medium-low and simmer, uncovered, for 30 minutes.

2. Strain the stock through a coarse wire sieve set over a large bowl. Cool to room temperature. (Cover and refrigerate for up to 3 days or freeze for up to 3 months.)

Makes about 2 quarts

chicken and asparagus with mustard-tarragon sauce

chicken and hominy chili

chicken breasts in jambalaya sauce

poached chicken breast in lemon-herb sauce

stir-fried chicken with orange-chile sauce

chicken, okra, and tomato stew

chicken and two mushroom ragù

thai chicken, mushroom, and basil stir-fry

chicken san juan

chicken sausage with white beans and rosemary

poached chicken in walnut-cilantro sauce

turkey and summer squash stir-fry

turkey and mushrooms in cream sauce

turkey sausage and black-eyed pea stew

FROM THE farm

this book was born out of

the daily pressure to create great meals fast.

For most home cooks, leisurely roasted meats

and simmered stews have to wait until a quiet

weekend comes up.

Weeknights require a quick plan of attack, and the easiest way for me to get dinner on the table often starts with a pot of rice. Most of the time, I pull out my skillet to whip up a fast stir-fry to spoon onto the grain. I can stir-fry many of my recipes so quickly that they are done at the same time as the rice! Even if you are a little slower with your knife than I am, you will still be doing all right in your battle against the kitchen clock.

Stir-fried meals do not always mean Asian food, although I have included many of my own favorite Chinese, Southeast Asian, Japanese, and Korean recipes. I often take the concept of the stir-fry—small pieces of meat and vegetables cooked quickly and combined in a light sauce—and apply it to other cuisines. You will find flavors of the Caribbean (Chicken San Juan), France (Chicken and Asparagus with Mustard-Tarragon Sauce), and Switzerland (Swiss Turkey and Mushrooms in Cream Sauce) in this chapter, as well as Asian dishes.

When preparing the ingredients for a stir-fry, try to follow the measurements given for the ingredients—at least by eye—so they will cook evenly. Obviously, carrots that are cut ¼ inch thick will cook more quickly than those cut ½ inch thick, so the sizes are important if all the ingredients are to be done at the same time. For tender stir-fried meat and poultry, slice against the grain into thin slices, about ½ inch thick. If you hold the knife at a slight angle, you will get wider slices instead of thin strips.

The most important part of stir-frying is the proper skillet. You do not need a wok, but you must have a skillet that is big enough to hold all of the ingredients for four to six servings. A large 12- to 14-inch skillet is perfect. If you don't own one already, you won't regret the purchase. Nonstick skillets allow you to use less oil than regular skillets. A wok or the relatively flat bottomed stir-fry skillet will also work, of course, keeping in mind that the curved sides of a wok make it difficult to brown pieces of meat and poultry that don't conform to the utensil's shape—which is why most stir-fries call for boneless meat.

Stir-fried foods are usually seared quickly to seal in juices. Always heat the empty skillet until it is very hot before adding the oil. Then, add the oil and tilt the skillet to coat the bottom of the pan. Let the oil get very hot before adding the other ingredients. Doing this ensures that the food will start to cook immediately upon contact with the skillet. Meat and poultry should never be crowded in the skillet, or the pieces will steam, not sear or brown. If necessary, cook them in two small batches, adding a little more oil to the skillet, if needed, for the second batch. Also, if stir-frying in a wok, remember that the food will be in contact with a larger cooking surface than in a skillet, since the wok is hot all the way up the sides. Therefore, the food should be tossed almost constantly with a wok paddle or large spoon to avoid burning.

chicken and asparagus with mustard-tarragon sauce

a good prepared mustard is a vital pantry staple. Sharp, white wine–based mustards used to be made only in Europe, particularly Dijon, France, but now the gourmet store shelves are crammed with domestic versions from mustard *meisters* from all over the United States. Try this with your favorite, maybe a herb-flavored brand. If using wild rice, allow more cooking time.

Can Be Cooked in Under 30 Minutes

French Rice or Steamed Rice (page 26), preferably made with long-grain rice or wild rice

¼ cup all-purpose flour

Salt

Freshly ground black pepper

1½ pounds boneless and skinless chicken breast, cut into strips 2 inches long and ½ inch wide

2 tablespoons vegetable oil

⅓ cup finely chopped shallots or scallions, white parts only

1 pound medium asparagus spears, trimmed and cut into 1-inch lengths

1 cup Homemade Chicken Broth (page 75) or low-sodium canned broth

⅓ cup dry vermouth or white wine

⅓ cup reduced-fat sour cream

2 tablespoons Dijon mustard

2 teaspoons chopped fresh tarragon or ¾ teaspoon dried tarragon

1. In a medium bowl or plastic bag, combine the flour, ¼ teaspoon salt and ¼ teaspoon pepper. Toss the chicken in the flour, shaking off the excess. In a large (12-inch) nonstick skillet, heat 1 tablespoon of the oil over medium-high heat. Add the chicken to the skillet. Cook, turning occa-sionally, until lightly browned, about 5 minutes. Transfer the chicken to a plate and set aside.

2. Add the remaining 1 tablespoon oil to the skillet. Add the shallots and stir until softened, about 30 seconds. Add the asparagus and ½ cup of the broth. Increase the heat to high. Cover and cook until just tender, about 3 minutes. Transfer the asparagus with the cooking liquid to a bowl and set aside.

3. Return the chicken strips to the skillet. Add the remaining ½ cup of the broth and the vermouth and bring to a simmer. Reduce the heat to medium-low and cook for 2 minutes. Remove the skillet from the heat.

4. In a small bowl, stir together the sour cream, mustard, and tarragon. Stir into the skillet. Return to the heat and cook until just heated through, but not boiling, about 1 minute. Stir in the asparagus and its liquid. Season with salt and pepper to taste.

5. Spoon the rice into individual soup bowls. Top with the chicken, asparagus, and sauce and serve immediately.

Makes 4 to 6 servings

chicken and hominy chili

Can Be Cooked in Under 30 Minutes

Beer Rice or Steamed Rice (page 26), preferably made with long-grain rice

1 tablespoon vegetable oil, or more as needed

1½ pounds boneless and skinless chicken thighs, cut into ¾-inch pieces

1 medium onion, chopped

1 medium red bell pepper, seeded and chopped

1 fresh chile, such as jalapeño, seeded and finely chopped

2 garlic cloves, minced

2 teaspoons chili powder

1 can (16 ounces) plum tomatoes in juice, juice reserved, coarsely chopped

1 can (16 ounces) hominy, drained and rinsed

1 cup Homemade Chicken Broth (page 75) or low-sodium canned broth

2 tablespoons yellow cornmeal

¼ teaspoon salt

Hot pepper sauce (optional)

Sour cream or plain yogurt, for garnish

everyone in the family will go for this mellow chili, even those with a low tolerance for spicy foods. If you can't find hominy, the large kernel corn with the big flavor, substitute two cups fresh or frozen corn kernels. The chili is also great served on wheat berries or bulgur.

1. In a large dutch oven or flameproof casserole, heat the oil over medium-high heat. Add the chicken and cook, stirring occasionally, until browned, about 6 minutes.

2. Add more oil to the dutch oven, if needed. Stir in the onion, bell pepper, chile pepper, and garlic. Cover and cook, stirring occasionally, until the vegetables soften, about 4 minutes. Add the chili powder and cook, uncovered, stirring often, until the juices are almost evaporated, about 2 minutes.

3. Add the tomatoes with their juices, the hominy, and chicken broth. Bring to a simmer and reduce the heat to medium-low. Cook, uncovered, until the chicken cooks through, about 5 minutes.

4. Transfer about ⅓ cup of the cooking juices to a small bowl. Add the cornmeal and stir until smooth. Stir the cornmeal mixture back into the sauce and cook until thickened, about 1 minute. Season with the salt and hot pepper sauce to taste.

5. Spoon the rice into individual soup bowls and top with the chili. Dollop each serving with sour cream and serve immediately.

Makes 4 to 6 servings

chicken breasts in jambalaya sauce

Steamed Rice (page 26), preferably
made with long-grain rice

1 tablespoon vegetable oil,
or more as needed

3 chicken breast halves with skin and
bones (9 ounces each), chopped
in half vertically to make 6 pieces

¼ teaspoon salt

¼ teaspoon freshly ground
black pepper

6 ounces smoked sausage, such as
andouille, chorizo, or kielbasa, cut
into ½-inch pieces

1 medium onion, chopped

1 medium bell pepper, seeded
and chopped

1 medium celery rib with leaves,
chopped

1 garlic clove, minced

1½ teaspoons Cajun Seasoning
(page 43)

1 cup canned crushed tomatoes

1 cup Homemade Chicken
Broth (page 75) or low-sodium
canned broth

8 ounces medium shrimp, peeled
and deveined

jambalaya, rice with a spicy tomato sauce filled with morsels of meat and seafood, is a rib-sticking Cajun classic. Some cooks make it with the rice cooked in the sauce, but that method can give unreliably sticky results. On my last trip to Baton Rouge, a local cook showed me how he prepares the rice separately and tops it with the tomato and meat sauce. He charges that the other way of making jambalaya is a sure way to ruin a pot with burned-on rice.

1. In a large dutch oven or flameproof casserole, heat the oil over medium-high heat. In batches, add the chicken breast pieces, skin side down, and cook, turning once, until lightly browned, about 5 minutes. Transfer to a plate, leaving the fat in the pan. Season the breasts with the salt and pepper and set aside.

2. Add more oil to the dutch oven, if needed. Add the sausage and reduce the heat to medium. Cook, stirring often, until the sausage is lightly browned, about 5 minutes. Add the onion, bell pepper, celery, and garlic. Cook, stirring often, until the vegetables soften, about 5 minutes. Stir in the Cajun Seasoning and cook for 1 minute.

3. Stir in the crushed tomatoes and chicken broth and bring to a simmer. Return the chicken breasts to the dutch oven and reduce the heat to medium-low. Simmer until the chicken shows no sign of pink when pierced in the thickest part, 15 to 20 minutes. Transfer the chicken to a plate and cover with aluminum foil to keep warm.

4. Skim any fat from the surface of the sauce. Stir in the shrimp and cook just until they turn pink and firm, about 3 minutes.

5. Spoon the rice onto individual dinner plates. Top each serving with the sauce and then with a chicken breast. Serve immediately.

Makes 4 to 6 servings

poached chicken breast in lemon-herb sauce

Can Be Cooked in Under 30 Minutes

Steamed Rice (page 26), preferably made with long-grain rice

1 tablespoon olive oil

3 medium carrots, cut into ¼-inch-thick rounds

1 medium zucchini, cut into ½-inch-thick half moons

4 scallions, white and green parts, chopped

1 garlic clove, minced

2 cups Homemade Chicken Broth (page 75) or low-sodium canned broth

6 boneless and skinless chicken breast halves (5 ounces each), rinsed and patted dry

Salt

Freshly ground white pepper

1 large egg, at room temperature

2 tablespoons fresh lemon juice

1 teaspoon cornstarch

2 teaspoons chopped fresh herbs, such as dill, chives, tarragon, or parsley, or 1 teaspoon chopped mint

boneless and skinless chicken breasts are popular because they make it possible to prepare an elegant entree in minutes. This recipe takes its cue from the famous Greek sauce, *avgolemono,* where a full-flavored broth is lightly thickened with egg and lemon juice. Vary the seasoning by using whatever fresh herb is available. When poaching chicken in broth, the proteins in the poultry often float to the broth's surface—rinsing the chicken first helps to keep the sauce smooth.

1. In a large dutch oven or flameproof casserole, heat the oil over medium heat. Add the carrots, zucchini, and scallions and cover. Cook, stirring often, until the vegetables soften, about 3 minutes. Add the garlic and cook 1 minute.

2. Add the chicken broth and bring to a boil over high heat. Season the chicken breasts with ¼ teaspoon salt and ⅛ teaspoon pepper. Add the chicken breasts and return the liquid to a boil. Reduce the heat to low and cover. Simmer until the chicken is firm and cooked through, about 12 minutes. Transfer the chicken breasts to a cutting board and cover with aluminum foil to keep warm.

3. In a small bowl, whisk the egg, lemon juice, cornstarch, and herbs to dissolve the cornstarch. Gradually stir about ½ cup of the hot cooking liquid into the egg mixture. Stirring constantly, pour the egg mixture into the cooking liquid. Cook just until the sauce is lightly thickened but not simmering, about 1 minute. Remove from the heat. Season with salt and pepper to taste.

4. Spoon the rice onto individual dinner plates and top with the sauce. Using a sharp knife, cut each breast diagonally into 4 or 5 thick slices, slip the knife under the sliced breast, and transfer to the bowl of rice, fanning out each breast slightly. Serve immediately.

Makes 4 to 6 servings

stir-fried chicken with orange-chile sauce

Can Be Cooked in Under 30 Minutes

Steamed Rice (page 26), preferably made with long-grain rice

3 tablespoons soy sauce

1 tablespoon plus 2 teaspoons corn starch

1 large egg white

1 teaspoon sugar

1½ pounds boneless and skinless chicken breast, cut into strips 2 inches long and ¾ inch wide

1 cup plus 2 tablespoons Homemade Chicken Broth (page 75) or low-sodium canned broth

¼ cup fresh orange juice

1 tablespoon black Chinese vinegar or balsamic vinegar

1 tablespoon hoisin sauce

1 tablespoon Asian dark sesame oil

Grated zest of 1 orange

2 tablespoons vegetable oil

3 scallions, white and green parts, chopped

1 tablespoon minced fresh ginger

it's challenging to duplicate restaurant-style Chinese food at home, since many popular dishes rely on deep-fried ingredients. I am happy to recreate my favorite dishes without deep-frying, making equally delicious meals without extra calories. A perfect example is this chicken in orange sauce. The addition of a colorful assortment of vegetables makes the dish more appealing than the typical batter-fried take-out version. As with most Chinese dishes, the ingredients list seems long, but once you get organized and start cooking, the meal will be ready before you know it.

6 whole small dried chiles, such as *japonés,* or ¼ teaspoon crushed red pepper

3 large garlic cloves, minced

2 large celery ribs, cut diagonally into ¼-inch-thick slices

1 large onion, cut into ¼-inch-thick half moons

1 large red bell pepper, seeded and cut into 1-inch pieces

1 can (15 oz.) baby corn, drained, rinsed, and cut in half horizontally

1. In a medium bowl, beat 1 tablespoon of the soy sauce, 1 tablespoon of the cornstarch, the egg white, and sugar with a fork until the cornstarch dissolves. Add the chicken breast strips and let stand for at least 15 minutes or up to 1 hour.

2. In a small bowl combine the remaining 2 tablespoons soy sauce and the remaining 2 teaspoons cornstarch, the broth, orange juice, vinegar, hoisin sauce, sesame oil, and orange zest. Set aside.

3. Heat a large (12-inch) nonstick skillet or large wok over medium-high heat. Add 1 tablespoon of the vegetable oil and heat until the oil is very hot. Add the chicken and stir-fry until cooked through, about 3 minutes. Transfer to a plate and set aside.

4. Heat the remaining 1 tablespoon vegetable oil in the skillet. Add the scallions, ginger, chiles, and garlic and stir-fry for 1 minute. Add the celery, onion, bell pepper, and baby corn. Stir-fry until crisp-tender, about 3 minutes.

5. Return the chicken to the skillet. Stir the orange juice mixture, add to the skillet, and bring to a simmer. Cook until the sauce is lightly thickened, about 1 minute.

6. Spoon the rice into individual bowls and top with the chicken stir-fry. Serve immediately.

Makes 4 to 6 servings

chicken, okra, and tomato stew

Can Be Cooked in Under 30 Minutes

Chicken-flavored Rice or Steamed Rice (page 26), preferably made with long-grain rice

6 ounces bacon, chopped

1½ pounds boneless, skinless chicken thighs, cut into 1-inch pieces

1 medium onion, chopped

1 medium green bell pepper, seeded and chopped

2 garlic cloves, minced

1 pound fresh okra, cut into ½-inch-thick rounds, or 1 package (12 ounces) sliced okra, thawed

1½ pounds ripe plum tomatoes, peeled, seeded, and chopped (see page 54), or 1 can (28 ounces) Italian plum tomatoes, drained and chopped

1½ cups Homemade Chicken Broth (page 75) or low-sodium canned broth

2 tablespoons yellow cornmeal

1 cup fresh or frozen corn kernels, thawed

2 tablespoons chopped dill

¼ teaspoon salt

¼ teaspoon freshly ground black pepper

either you like okra and its slick, gluey juices or you don't. The trick is to cook okra past its crisp stage so it loses some of its gooeyness while still retaining its bright green color. I have taken some liberties with a traditional gumbo (named for the Angolan word for okra) and come up with a mild version, accented with corn and seasoned with dill and bacon. The sauce is thickened with cornmeal, which soaks up the juices, adding both body and flavor.

1. In a large dutch oven or flameproof casserole, cook the bacon over medium heat until crisp, about 4 minutes. Using a slotted spoon, transfer the bacon to a paper towel-lined plate. Pour off the bacon fat into a small bowl. Return 1 tablespoon of the fat to the dutch oven.

2. Add the chicken and cook, turning occasionally, until cooked through, about 7 minutes. Transfer the chicken to a plate and set aside.

3. Add the onion, bell pepper, and garlic, adding some of the bacon fat, if needed. Cook, stirring often, until the vegetables soften, about 4 minutes. Add the okra, tomatoes, and ½ cup of the broth. Cover and cook, stirring often, until the okra is tender, about 10 minutes.

4. Return the chicken to the dutch oven. In a small bowl, whisk together the cornmeal and the remaining 1 cup broth. Stir into the stew with the corn and dill. Bring to a simmer. Cook until the sauce is slightly thickened, about 1 minute. Season with the salt and pepper.

5. Spoon the rice into individual soup bowls and top with the stew. Crumble the bacon, sprinkle on the stew, and serve immediately.

Makes 4 to 6 servings

chicken and two mushroom ragù

*Boiled Rice (page 27), preferably
made with Italian rice*

1 ounce (1 cup) dried porcini
mushrooms

Nonstick vegetable oil cooking spray

1¼ pounds ground chicken

10 ounces fresh mushrooms, sliced

1 medium onion, chopped

1 medium carrot, finely chopped

1 medium celery rib with leaves,
finely chopped

1 can (16 ounces) plum tomatoes,
drained and coarsely chopped

⅓ cup dry vermouth

2 tablespoons tomato paste

1 tablespoon chopped fresh rosemary
or 1 teaspoon dried rosemary

½ cup heavy cream

½ teaspoon salt

¼ teaspoon freshly ground
black pepper

ragù, the meaty Italian tomato sauce, has many recipes. Each one comes with dire warnings not to vary from that particular version in any way whatsoever, pitting pancetta against chicken livers or cream versus milk. While ground chicken is definitely nontraditional, it is the foundation for one of my most requested sauces, equally favored on rice, polenta, pasta, or even mashed potatoes.

1. In a small bowl, soak the dried mushrooms in 1 cup hot water until softened, about 30 minutes. The mushrooms can also be microwaved on High (100%) for 30 seconds and then left to soak for 5 minutes. Lift out the mushrooms, rinse quickly under cold water to remove grit, and coarsely chop. Set aside.

2. Strain the soaking liquid through a paper towel–lined sieve into a small saucepan. Bring the liquid to a boil over high heat and cook until reduced to about 3 tablespoons, 5 to 7 minutes. Set aside.

3. Spray a large dutch oven or flameproof casserole with vegetable oil spray and place over medium-high heat. Add the ground chicken, soaked mushrooms, fresh mushrooms, onion, carrot, and celery. Cook, breaking up the chicken with a wooden spoon, until the meat loses its pink color and the vegetables soften, about 8 minutes.

4. Add the tomatoes, reduced mushroom liquid, vermouth, tomato paste, and rosemary, stirring to dissolve the tomato paste. Bring to a simmer and reduce the heat to low. Simmer, uncovered, until the tomato juices thicken, about 20 minutes. Stir in the heavy cream and simmer for 5 minutes. Season with the salt and pepper.

5. Spoon the rice into individual soup bowls, top with the ragù, and serve immediately.

Variation

Lowfat Chicken and Two Mushroom Ragù: Substitute ½ cup evaporated skim milk for the heavy cream. Stir into the sauce and heat through without boiling.

Makes 4 to 6 servings

thai chicken, mushroom, and basil stir-fry

Can Be Cooked in Under 30 Minutes

Steamed Rice (page 26), preferably made with jasmine rice

2 tablespoons vegetable oil

1½ pounds boneless and skinless chicken breast, cut into strips 2 inches long and ½ inch wide

10 ounces mushrooms, sliced

2 tablespoons minced shallots or scallions, white parts only

1½ tablespoons minced fresh ginger

1 tablespoon thinly sliced fresh chile rounds, from 2 small Thai chiles, or 1 medium jalapeño

3 garlic cloves, minced

1½ cups Homemade Chicken Broth (page 75) or low-sodium canned broth

1½ tablespoons Asian fish sauce (see page 39)

1½ teaspoons sugar

¾ cup coarsely chopped basil

¼ teaspoon crushed red pepper

Salt

the sensational flavors of Southeast Asia are quickly asserting themselves in the American kitchen. This stir-fry has become popular with my friends who love Thai cuisine but want to cook with easy-to-find ingredients. Even though many supermarkets now carry Asian fish sauce, you can make an acceptable substitute from pantry items.

1. In a large (12-inch) nonstick skillet, heat 1 tablespoon of the oil over medium-high heat. Add the chicken breast and cook, stirring often, until lightly browned, 4 to 5 minutes. Transfer to a plate and set aside.

2. Add the remaining 1 tablespoon oil to the skillet and heat. Add the mushrooms, shallots, ginger, chiles, and garlic. Cook, stirring often, until the mushrooms are lightly browned, about 5 minutes. Stir in the broth, fish sauce, and sugar. Bring to a simmer.

3. Return the chicken to the skillet and stir in the basil. Cook until the sauce has reduced slightly, about 2 minutes. Season with crushed red pepper and salt to taste, keeping in mind that the fish sauce and broth may have added enough salt of their own.

4. Spoon the rice into individual soup bowls, top with the stir-fry, and serve immediately.

Makes 4 to 6 servings

chicken
san juan

Can Be Cooked in Under 30 Minutes

*Saffron Rice or Steamed Rice
(pages 26), preferably made with
medium-grain rice*

1 tablespoon olive oil

1½ pounds boneless and skinless
chicken breast, cut into strips
2 inches long and ½ inch wide

1 medium onion, chopped

1 medium red bell pepper, seeded
and chopped

2 garlic cloves, minced

1 teaspoon dried oregano

1 bay leaf

1¾ cups Homemade Chicken
Broth (page 75) or low-sodium
canned broth

1 cup thawed frozen peas

½ cup medium pimiento-stuffed
green olives

½ teaspoon sweet
Hungarian paprika

2 teaspoons cornstarch

¼ teaspoon salt

¼ teaspoon freshly ground
black pepper

Chopped cilantro, for garnish

puerto Rico's heritage of simple cooking combines Spanish flavors and Caribbean ingredients. One of the most popular island meals is *arroz con pollo,* a baked rice and chicken casserole; it translates perfectly into a very quick sauce to spoon over rice. For a change of pace, try this over quinoa.

1. In a large (12-inch) nonstick skillet, heat the oil over medium-high heat. Add the chicken and cook, turning occasionally, until lightly browned, about 5 minutes.

2. Add the onion, red pepper, garlic, oregano, and bay leaf. Cover and cook until the vegetables soften, about 4 minutes. Stir in the chicken broth, peas, olives, and paprika and bring to a simmer. Reduce the heat to low and simmer for 2 minutes.

3. Transfer about ¼ cup of the cooking liquid into a small bowl. Add the cornstarch and stir until dissolved. Stir the cornstarch mixture into the skillet and cook until the liquid is slightly thickened, about 1 minute. Season with the salt and pepper. Discard the bay leaf.

4. Spoon the rice into individual soup bowls and top with the chicken and sauce. Sprinkle with the cilantro and serve immediately.

Makes 4 to 6 servings

chicken sausage with white beans and rosemary

Can Be Cooked in Under 30 Minutes

Steamed Rice (page 26), preferably made with long-grain rice

1 pound hot or sweet chicken or turkey Italian sausage

1 tablespoon olive oil

1 medium onion, chopped

1 medium red bell pepper, seeded and chopped

2 garlic cloves, minced

1 cup Homemade Chicken Broth (page 75) or low-sodium canned broth

½ cup dry white wine

1 tablespoon chopped fresh rosemary or 1½ teaspoons dried rosemary

2 cans (15 ounces each) white kidney beans (cannellini)

¼ teaspoon salt

⅛ teaspoon freshly ground black pepper

my kitchen cupboard is full of beans—black, white, pink, red, and so on through the color spectrum. When I have the time, I do simmer up dried beans, but for everyday, short-order cooking, canned beans are fine. This is a Tuscan version of the worldwide pairing of beans and rice.

1. Pierce the sausage all over with a fork. Place in a medium saucepan and add enough cold water to cover. Bring to a boil over medium-high heat. Reduce the heat to medium-low. Simmer, uncovered, until the sausage is firm, about 8 minutes. Transfer the sausage to a plate and cool. Cut the sausage into ½-inch-thick rounds and set aside.

2. In a large Dutch oven or flameproof casserole, heat the oil over medium heat. Add the onion, bell pepper, and garlic. Cook, stirring often, until the vegetables soften, about 4 minutes.

3. Stir in the broth, wine, and rosemary. Bring to a simmer and reduce the heat to medium-low. Simmer, uncovered, for 5 minutes. Stir in the beans and sausage rounds and simmer for 10 minutes, until the beans are hot. Season with the salt and pepper.

4. Spoon the rice into individual soup bowls, top with the beans and sausage, and serve immediately.

Makes 4 to 6 servings

poached chicken in walnut-cilantro sauce

Steamed Rice (page 26), preferably made with long-grain rice

Chicken and Broth

1 tablespoon vegetable oil

1 chicken (4½ pounds), cut into 2 wings, 2 drumstick/thigh portions, 2 breasts, and 1 back, with giblets (do not use the liver)

1 medium onion, chopped

1 medium carrot, chopped

1 medium celery rib with leaves, chopped

2½ quarts water, or more if needed

1 teaspoon salt

½ teaspoon dried thyme

1 bay leaf

¼ teaspoon whole black peppercorns

When I need a fresh batch of homemade broth, I often prepare a recipe that yields a main course and a big pot of broth at the same time. This chicken in an unusual walnut sauce, for instance, depends on an excellent chicken broth for its success, making it the perfect opportunity to stock up on stock. Since the dish is made with a large, meaty chicken instead of bones only, the normally long simmering time is drastically reduced. You can serve the chicken either hot with the peas and sauce over rice or kasha or slightly chilled on a bed of lettuce.

1. To make the chicken and broth, heat the oil in a large pot or flameproof casserole over medium-high heat. In batches, add the chicken and cook, turning occasionally, until browned, about 5 minutes. Transfer the chicken to a plate.

2. Add the onion, carrot, and celery to the pot and reduce the heat to medium. Cover and cook until the vegetables soften, about 6 minutes. Return the chicken to the pot and pour in enough water to cover. Bring to a boil over high heat, skimming off any foam that rises to the surface. Add the salt, thyme, bay leaf, and peppercorns. Reduce the heat to low and simmer until the chicken is cooked through, about 40 minutes. Transfer the chicken wings, leg portions and breasts to a plate, leaving the back and giblets to continue simmering.

3. Let the chicken pieces stand until cool enough to handle, about 10 minutes. Pull the meat off the bones into bite-size pieces and set aside. Return the chicken skin and bones to the pot and continue to simmer until the broth is richly flavored, about 45 minutes.

4. Strain the broth through a colander set over a large bowl and discard the solids. Let the stock stand for 5 minutes, then skim off the fat from the surface. Reserve 2½ cups broth for the sauce.

Walnut-Cilantro Sauce

1 tablespoon walnut or olive oil

1 small onion, chopped

1 garlic clove, minced

1 cup fresh bread crumbs

1 cup walnuts, finely chopped

2½ cups reserved chicken broth

1 tablespoon cider vinegar

¼ cup chopped cilantro

2 cups fresh or frozen peas

½ teaspoon salt

¼ teaspoon freshly ground
  black pepper

Chopped cilantro, for garnish

5. To make the sauce, heat the oil in a medium (9-inch) nonstick skillet over medium heat. Add the onion and cook, stirring often, until golden, about 5 minutes. Add the garlic and cook for 1 minute. Add the bread crumbs and cook, stirring often, until lightly browned, about 3 minutes. Stir in the walnuts, 2 cups of the broth, vinegar, and cilantro and bring to a simmer. Reduce the heat to medium-low and cook, stirring often, until the sauce is thickened but pourable, about 15 minutes. If necessary, add a little water to the sauce to keep it from drying out.

6. To serve, cook the peas in lightly salted water until tender, about 4 minutes for fresh peas and 2 minutes for frozen. Drain and keep warm.

7. Stir the chicken into the sauce (the sauce will thicken). Add enough of the remaining ½ cup broth to thin the sauce to the consistency of thick heavy cream. Cook over low heat, stirring often, until the chicken is heated through, about 3 minutes. Season with the salt and pepper.

8. Spoon the rice into soup bowls and top with the chicken and sauce. Sprinkle with the cilantro and serve immediately.

Homemade Chicken Broth

For a supply of homemade broth, proceed through Step 4. Cool the remaining broth to room temperature, then refrigerate or freeze in 2-cup containers. (The broth can be stored for up to 3 days, covered, in the refrigerator, or for 3 months in the freezer.) Makes about 2 quarts chicken broth.

Makes 4 to 6 servings

turkey and summer squash stir-fry

Can Be Cooked in Under 30 Minutes

Steamed Rice (page 26), preferably made with long-grain rice

3 tablespoons soy sauce

3 tablespoons rice wine or dry vermouth

2 teaspoons sugar

1 pound turkey cutlets, cut into strips 3 inches long and ½ inch wide

2 tablespoons vegetable oil

1 large onion, cut into ½-inch-thick half moons

3 scallions, white and green parts, chopped

1 tablespoon minced fresh ginger

1 garlic clove, minced

2 medium (1 pound) zucchini, cut into ¼-inch-thick half moons

2 medium (1 pound) yellow summer squash, cut into ¼-inch-thick half moons

½ cup Homemade Chicken Broth (page 75) or low-sodium canned broth

1 teaspoon cornstarch

this is a very straightforward stir-fry recipe that uses its marinade as the base for the sauce. It is equally good with pork or chicken.

1. In a medium bowl, combine the soy sauce, rice wine, and sugar. Add the turkey strips and marinate at room temperature for 15 to 30 minutes.

2. Heat a large (12-inch) nonstick skillet or wok over high heat. Add 1 tablespoon of the oil and heat until hot. Add the onion and stir-fry for 1 minute. Stir in the scallions, ginger, and garlic. Add the zucchini and yellow squash and cook, stirring often, until crisp-tender, about 4 minutes. Transfer to a bowl and set aside.

3. Drain the turkey strips, reserving the marinade. Add the chicken broth and cornstarch to the marinade and whisk to dissolve. Set aside.

4. Add the remaining 1 tablespoon oil to the skillet and reduce the heat to medium-high. Add the turkey strips to the skillet and cook, stirring often, until the turkey is cooked through, about 4 minutes.

5. Return the vegetables to the skillet. Stir the marinade mixture, add to the skillet, and bring to a boil. Cook until the sauce is thickened, about 1 minute.

6. Spoon the rice into individual soup bowls, top with the turkey, vegetables, and sauce, and serve immediately.

Makes 4 to 6 servings

turkey and mushrooms in cream sauce

Can Be Cooked in Under 30 Minutes

French Rice or Steamed Rice (page 26), preferably made with long-grain rice

¼ cup all-purpose flour

Salt

Freshly ground black pepper

1 pound turkey cutlets, cut into ¾-inch squares

1½ tablespoons vegetable oil

1 tablespoon unsalted butter

⅓ cup finely chopped shallots or scallions, white parts only

10 ounces mushrooms, sliced

1 tablespoon fresh lemon juice

1 cup dry white wine

1 cup heavy cream

Chopped chives or parsley, for garnish

One summer, I spent a blissfully sweet few weeks studying chocolate confectionery skills in Switzerland, where I first sampled the national dish, minced veal and mushrooms in cream sauce. Back home, I make it with turkey cutlets, which are often easier to find and less expensive than veal, but you can use veal scaloppine, if you insist on authenticity. Lavish in flavor yet simple to prepare, this is created with a few well-chosen ingredients without a herb or spice in sight. With its carefree use of heavy cream, it probably won't become everyday fare for Americans, so save this recipe for indulgent special occasions.

1. In a medium bowl or plastic bag, combine the flour, ¼ teaspoon salt and ¼ teaspoon pepper. Toss the turkey in the flour, shaking off the excess. In a large (12-inch) nonstick skillet, heat the oil over medium heat. Be careful: Turkey is very lean and will toughen if the heat is too high. Add the turkey to the skillet. Cook, turning occasionally, until the turkey is lightly browned, about 6 minutes. Transfer the turkey to a plate and set aside.

2. Add the butter to the skillet and melt. Add the shallots and cook, stirring often, until softened, about 1 minute. Add the mushrooms and lemon juice and stir well. Cover and cook until the mushrooms give off their juices, about 3 minutes. Uncover, increase the heat to high, and cook until the mushroom liquid evaporates, about 3 minutes.

3. Pour in the wine and boil, uncovered, until slightly reduced, about 2 minutes. Add the heavy cream and cook until the liquid has reduced by about one-fourth, 5 to 7 minutes. Return the turkey to the skillet and cook until the sauce is lightly thickened, about 1 minute. Season with salt and pepper to taste.

4. Spoon the rice into individual soup bowls and top with the turkey, mushrooms, and sauce. Sprinkle with the chives and serve immediately.

Makes 4 to 6 servings

turkey sausage and black-eyed pea stew

Can Be Cooked in Under 30 Minutes

Steamed Rice (page 26), preferably made with long-grain rice

1 tablespoon vegetable oil

8 ounces hot turkey sausage or pork sausage, casings removed

1 medium onion, chopped

2 medium celery rib with leaves, chopped

2 large garlic cloves, minced

2 tablespoons chopped parsley

2 teaspoons chopped fresh sage or ¾ teaspoon dried sage

3 cups unthawed frozen black-eyed peas

1¾ cups Homemade Chicken Broth (page 75) or low-sodium canned broth

1 tablespoon plus 1 teaspoon all-purpose flour

1 teaspoon Cajun Seasoning (page 43)

3 ripe plum tomatoes, peeled, seeded, and chopped (see page 54)

¼ teaspoon salt

Hot pepper sauce (optional)

In this dish, the earthy flavor of humble black-eyed peas is dressed up with sausage, spices, and tomatoes. In my produce market (well north of the Mason-Dixon line), fresh black-eyed peas are rare, so I use the frozen variety. However, in the summer down South, farmers' markets are filled with bushels of just-picked peas in the pod, which can be shelled on the spot by strange-looking contraptions that look like something out of Rube Goldberg. If you are a true child of the South, you may like this over grits.

1. In a large dutch oven or flameproof casserole, heat the oil over medium heat. Add the sausage, onion, and celery, breaking up the sausage with a spoon, until the sausage loses its pink color, about 5 minutes. Add the garlic, parsley, and sage and stir for 1 minute.

2. Add the black-eyed peas and ¼ cup of the broth. Cover and reduce the heat to medium-low. Cook until the peas are tender, about 12 minutes.

3. Sprinkle with the flour and Cajun Seasoning and stir constantly for 1 minute. Stir in the remaining 1½ cups broth and the tomatoes. Simmer until the tomatoes are heated through, about 3 minutes. Season with the salt and hot pepper sauce to taste.

4. Spoon the rice into individual soup bowls, top with the black-eyed peas and sauce, and serve immediately.

Makes 4 to 6 servings

korean beef on fiery chinese cabbage

beef and shiitake mushrooms in sukiyaki sauce

stir-fried beef with tomatoes in tangy sauce

sirloin and black bean chili

beef shanks with chianti and gremolata

ground beef and squash picadillo

mongolian lamb with broccoli

middle eastern lamb sauce with pine nuts and currants

lamb chops with zuni vegetable sauce

pork tenderloin with curried fruit sauce

pork and mushroom goulash

smoked pork chops with beer-braised cabbage

pork fajita stir-fry

new york diner fried rice

FROM THE range

even though poultry,

fish, and vegetables continue to show up on the

American table more often than ever, many

people still enjoy tucking into a meat meal.

The most familiar way of serving meat on rice is an Asian-style stir-fry, but there's more than one way to satisfy a carnivore.

Consider the Korean Beef on Fiery Chinese Cabbage, where marinated steak is sliced and served over chile-seasoned cabbage and rice. You could still eat that with chopsticks. But, the simmered Lamb Chops with Zuni Vegetable Sauce is strictly knife-and-fork fare. Ground lamb makes an appearance in an unusually seasoned sauce (Middle Eastern Lamb Sauce with Pine Nuts and Currants) and if you love stew as much as I do, Beef Shanks with Chianti and Gremolata should become a favorite. It also provides the bonus of a fine beef broth to have on hand to enrich other dishes.

The variety of techniques in this chapter reflects how different cuts of meat cook, regardless of whether it's beef, lamb, or pork. Some cuts need moist, slow cooking to become tender. Others can be quickly broiled or stir-fried. Few cuts are good prepared both ways. If you want to substitute one cut or type of meat for another, be careful to choose one that will benefit from the type of cooking in the recipe. London broil could be substituted for sirloin in Korean Beef on Fiery Chinese Cabbage, for example, but if loin lamb chops were used instead of shoulder chops in the Lamb Chops with Zuni Vegetable Sauce, the loin chops would end up dry and tasteless—and be a waste of an expensive cut of meat. Ask your butcher for advice before you make any substitutions.

korean beef on fiery chinese cabbage

Steamed Rice (page 26), preferably made with long-grain rice

Korean Marinade

1 tablespoon sesame seed

⅓ cup soy sauce

2 scallions, finely chopped

1 tablespoon sugar

1 tablespoon Asian dark sesame oil

1 tablespoon minced fresh ginger

¼ teaspoon crushed red pepper

1½ pounds sirloin steak, trimmed, about ¾ inch thick

Spicy Chinese Cabbage

1 medium (1½ pounds) Chinese (napa) cabbage

1 tablespoon vegetable oil

3 scallions, chopped

1 tablespoon minced fresh ginger

3 garlic cloves, minced

½ cup Homemade Chicken Broth (page 75) or low-sodium canned broth

½ teaspoon salt

¼ teaspoon ground hot pepper

2 medium carrots, shredded

2 tablespoons rice vinegar

a couple of years ago, I was asked to teach American cooking classes in Korea, and I think I learned as much about my students' cuisine as they did about mine. I went wild over their grilled meats, many marinated in a soy sauce–sesame mixture so thick it is almost a paste—kind of a high-octane teriyaki. All Korean meals are accompanied with kimchi, a fiery pickle often made with Chinese cabbage. I don't make my own kimchi anymore (it filled my kitchen with some pretty startling aromas), but I do make a peppery cabbage stir-fry to act as a foil for grilled or broiled marinated steak, all served over freshly cooked rice.

1. To make the marinade, heat a medium skillet over medium heat. Add the sesame seeds and cook, stirring almost constantly, until toasted and golden brown, about 3 minutes. Transfer to a plate to cool. In a mortar or on the work surface using a heavy skillet, coarsely crush the sesame seeds. Place in a large shallow dish.

2. Add the remaining marinade ingredients and stir well to combine. Add the steak and rub some of the marinade ingredients over the top. Cover with plastic wrap and refrigerate for as long as possible, at least 1 hour or up to 8 hours.

3. To make the spicy cabbage, core and cut crosswise into ½-inch strips. Heat a large (12-inch) nonstick skillet or wok over medium-high heat until hot. Add the oil, tilt the skillet to coat the bottom, and heat until the oil is very hot. Add the scallions, ginger, and garlic and stir-fry until very fragrant, about 30 seconds. Add the cabbage, chicken broth, salt, and hot pepper. Cook, uncovered, stirring often,

until the cabbage stalks are translucent and crisp-tender, about 5 minutes. Stir in the carrots and vinegar. Remove from heat, cover, and keep warm.

4. Position a broiler rack 6 inches from the source of heat and preheat the broiler. Remove the meat from the marinade, reserving the marinade. Broil the meat, turning once, until cooked to desired doneness, about 7 minutes for medium-rare.

5. Meanwhile, pour the marinade into a small saucepan and bring to a boil over low heat. Simmer for 2 minutes. Set aside.

6. If necessary, reheat the cabbage. Cut the meat diagonally across the grain into ½-inch-thick slices. Spoon the rice into soup bowls. Top with the cabbage, and then the sliced meat. Pour some of the marinade over each serving of meat, and serve immediately.

Makes 4 to 6 servings

beef and shiitake mushrooms in sukiyaki sauce

Can Be Cooked in Under 30 Minutes

Steamed Rice (page 26), preferably
    made with Japanese-style sushi rice

2 tablespoons vegetable oil

1½ pounds sirloin steak,
    well-trimmed, sliced diagonally across
    the grain about ¼ inch thick

1 onion, cut into ¼-inch-thick half moons

4 ounces shiitake mushrooms,
    stems discarded, caps cut into
    ¼-inch strips

1½ cups Homemade Beef
    Broth (page 91) or low-sodium
    canned broth

2 tablespoons soy sauce

¼ cup sake or dry sherry

1 teaspoon sugar

1 bunch (8 ounces) spinach, stems
    discarded, leaves stacked and cut
    across into ½-inch strips

5 ounces firm tofu, cut into cubes

2 cups (6 ounces) bean sprouts

1 tablespoon plus 2 teaspoons
    cornstarch, dissolved in
    2 tablespoons water

¼ teaspoon freshly ground
    black pepper

now there are sushi restaurants all over the United States, but when I was growing up in San Francisco, a trip to a Japanese restaurant was considered the ultimate in refined adult dining, and a rare treat. The private dining rooms, the waitresses' ornate robes, the strange custom of taking off one's shoes in the restaurant—it was a brief entrance into a hushed, foreign world. My favorite dish was sukiyaki, its rich broth filled with beef, mushrooms, and tofu (yes, I even ate the tofu, partly because I was afraid that turning it down would prove my ignorance of Japanese culture and cuisine, but I also liked it). There are few meals that are quicker and easier to make than this dish, based on my old culinary friend.

1. Heat a large (12-inch) nonstick skillet or wok over high heat. Add 1½ teaspoons of the oil and heat until very hot. Add half of the beef. Cook, stirring often, until seared on all sides, about 3 minutes. Transfer to a plate and set aside. Repeat with another 1½ teaspoons oil and the remaining beef.

2. Add the remaining 1 tablespoon oil to the skillet and heat. Add the onion and mushrooms and stir-fry until the onion softens, about 3 minutes.

3. Stir in the beef broth, soy sauce, sake, and sugar and bring to a boil. Add the spinach, tofu, and bean sprouts and cook until the spinach is wilted, about 1 minute. Stir the cornstarch mixture, add to the skillet, and cook until the sauce is slightly thickened. Season with the pepper.

4. Spoon the rice into individual dinner plates, top with the beef-vegetable mixture, and serve immediately.

Makes 4 to 6 servings

stir-fried beef with tomatoes in tangy sauce

Can Be Cooked in Under 30 Minutes

Steamed Rice (page 26), preferably made with long-grain rice

2 ½ tablespoons soy sauce

1 ½ tablespoons rice wine or dry sherry

3 ½ teaspoons cornstarch

1 ½ pounds flank or skirt steak, cut diagonally into strips 2 inches long and ½ inch thick

½ cup Homemade Chicken Broth (page 75) or canned low-sodium broth

¼ cup ketchup

1 tablespoon cider vinegar

2 teaspoons sugar

¼ teaspoon freshly ground black pepper

2 tablespoons vegetable oil, or more as needed

1 large onion, cut into ½-inch-thick half moons

1 large green bell pepper, seeded and cut into ¾-inch pieces

3 medium celery ribs, cut diagonally into ¼-inch-thick slices

2 garlic cloves, minced

2 medium tomatoes, cut into eighths

One of the best things about growing up Californian was an early exposure to Chinese cooking. Practically every town had a family-owned Cantonese restaurant offering great food, carefully prepared. My great-aunt Soulima would take me every week to our local chop suey palace, where she would always order her favorite— tomato beef. I miss being able to walk into just about any Chinese restaurant and get simple food like this. Now, I make it at home with happy memories.

1. In a medium bowl, mix 1 ½ tablespoons of the soy sauce, the rice wine, and 1 ½ teaspoons of the cornstarch. Add the beef strips and toss. Let stand for 15 to 30 minutes.

2. In a small bowl, combine the remaining 1 tablespoon soy sauce, the chicken broth, ketchup, vinegar, sugar, and pepper. Add the remaining 2 teaspoons cornstarch and whisk to combine. Set aside.

3. Heat a large (12-inch) skillet or wok over medium-high heat until hot. Add 1 tablespoon of the oil, swirl to coat the bottom of the skillet, and heat until the oil is very hot. In 2 batches, adding more oil as needed, cook the beef strips, turning occasionally, until browned, about 4 minutes. Transfer to a plate and set aside.

4. Add the remaining 1 tablespoon oil to the skillet and heat until very hot. Add the onion, bell pepper, celery, and garlic. Stir-fry until the vegetables are crisp-tender, about 3 minutes.

5. Return the beef to the skillet. Stir the broth mixture and add to the skillet with the tomatoes. Bring to a boil, stirring gently until the tomatoes are heated through, about 1 minute.

6. Spoon rice into individual bowls. Top with beef and tomatoes and serve immediately.

Makes 4 to 6 servings

sirloin and black bean chili

Can Be Cooked in Under 30 Minutes

Beer Rice or Steamed Rice (page 26), preferably made with long-grain rice

2 tablespoons olive oil, or more as needed

1½ pounds sirloin steak, ¾-inch thick, cut into cubes

1 large onion, chopped

1 medium green bell pepper, seeded and chopped

3 garlic cloves, minced

2 tablespoons chili powder

2 teaspoons cumin seed, toasted and crushed (see page 124)

1 teaspoon dried oregano

1 cup Homemade Beef Broth (page 91) or low-sodium canned broth

1 can (8 ounces) tomato sauce

1 can (15 ounces) black beans, drained and rinsed

¼ teaspoon salt

¼ teaspoon freshly ground black pepper

Shredded cheddar cheese, sour cream, and chopped scallions, for garnish

many Texans simmer their chili for hours, but that's often because they're using tough cuts of beef that need to take their own sweet time to cook until tender. Using a cut like sirloin gives you a meaty taste without long cooking. In fact, you shouldn't cook it too long, or it will dry out. This chili is also very good on corn grits or cooked wheat berries, spelt, or kamut.

1. In a large dutch oven or flameproof casserole, heat 1 tablespoon of the oil over high heat. In 2 batches, add the steak and cook, turning occasionally, until seared, about 5 minutes. Transfer to a plate and set aside. Add more oil if needed.

2. Add the remaining 1 tablespoon oil to the dutch oven and heat. Stir in the onion, bell pepper, and garlic and cover. Reduce the heat to medium and cook until the onion softens, about 5 minutes.

3. Return the steak to the dutch oven. Add the chili powder, cumin, and oregano and stir for 1 minute. Stir in the beef broth and tomato sauce, bring to a simmer and cover. Reduce the heat to medium-low and simmer for 5 minutes. Stir in the black beans and cook until heated through, about 3 minutes. Season with the salt and pepper.

4. Spoon the rice into individual serving bowls. Top with the chili and serve immediately. Pass bowls of cheese, sour cream, and scallions at the table.

Makes 4 to 6 servings

beef shanks with chianti and gremolata

Steamed Rice (page 26), preferably made with long-grain rice

Beef and Broth

1 tablespoon olive oil, or more if needed

4 pounds beef shanks, sawed cross-wise into 1½-inch-thick slices

2 medium onions, quartered

2 medium carrots, cut into ½-inch rounds

2 medium celery ribs with leaves, cut into ½-inch-thick slices

2 medium turnips, peeled and cut into ¾-inch pieces

1 large tomato, peeled, seeded, and coarsely chopped (see page 54)

2 garlic cloves, crushed

2½ quarts water, or more if needed

1 teaspoon dried thyme

1 bay leaf

1 teaspoon salt

¼ teaspoon freshly ground black pepper

most of the recipes in this book are weeknight fare—fast meals for busy cooks. The weekend is becoming the quality time set aside for more leisurely, long-simmered foods like this aromatic beef stew. Slow-cooked food must not disappear from our frenzied lives, just be rescheduled! In order to get a full return on invested time, make stews in a two-step process, producing not only a main course but a supply of homemade broth to use in other recipes. Like this recipe, Poached Chicken in Walnut-Cilantro Sauce (page 74), and Old-Fashioned Vegetable-Rice Soup (page 126) make both a main course and extra broth.

Bone-in beef shanks are perfect for this procedure, as their high gelatin content keeps the meat moist; it doesn't fall apart or dry out at all during cooking. The result is an absolutely terrific broth with the added attraction of poached marrow to enrich the sauce. If you can, make the stew early in the day—or even the night before serving—so the flavors can mellow.

1. To make the beef and broth, heat the oil in a large pot or flameproof casserole over medium-high heat. In batches, add the beef shanks and cook, turning once, until browned, about 5 minutes. Transfer to a plate and set aside.

2. Add more oil to the pot if needed and reduce the heat to medium. Add the onions, carrots, celery, and turnips. Cover and cook, stirring often, until the vegetables soften, about 10 minutes. Add the tomato and garlic and cook for 1 minute.

3. Return the beef to the pot. Pour in the water, adding more water to cover the meat if needed. Bring to a boil over high heat, skimming off any foam that rises to the surface. Add the thyme, bay leaf,

salt, and pepper. Reduce the heat to low and partially cover. Simmer until the meat is very tender, about 2 hours.

4. Transfer the meat to a plate. Strain the broth through a colander set over a large bowl and discard the bay leaf. Let the broth stand for 5 minutes, then skim off the clear fat from the surface. Reserve 2 cups of the broth.

5. Return the vegetables to the pot. Remove the meat and marrow from the bones, discarding the bones and gristle. Cut the meat into large pieces and return to the pot. Chop the marrow into ½-inch pieces and set aside.

Gremolata

2 tablespoons chopped parsley

Grated zest of 1 orange

Grated zest of 1 lemon

2 large garlic cloves, minced

Stew

3 tablespoons unsalted butter

3 tablespoons all-purpose flour

2 cups reserved beef broth

½ cup red wine, such as Chianti

2 tablespoons chopped parsley

¼ teaspoon salt

¼ teaspoon freshly ground black pepper

6. To make the gremolata, combine the parsley, orange zest, lemon zest, and garlic in a small bowl and set aside.

7. To make the stew, in a heavy-bottomed medium saucepan over medium-low heat, melt the butter. Whisk in the flour and let bubble, whisking often, until lightly browned, about 2 minutes. Whisk in the broth and red wine and bring to a simmer. Reduce the heat to very low and simmer until thickened, about 30 minutes. During the last 10 minutes of simmering, stir in half of the gremolata.

8. Stir the sauce into the meat and vegetables in the pot. Bring to a simmer over medium heat, then reduce the heat to low. Simmer for 10 minutes. Stir in the reserved marrow. Season with the salt and pepper. Transfer the stew to a heated serving dish.

9. Serve the stew over the rice, sprinkling each serving with a little of the remaining gremolata.

Variations

Lamb Shanks with Chianti and Gremolata: Substitute 4 pounds lamb shanks, sawed into 1½-inch-thick slices, for the beef shanks. Refrigerate or freeze the extra broth.

Veal Shanks with White Wine and Gremolata: Substitute 4 pounds veal shanks, sawed into 1½-inch-thick slices, for the beef shanks, and ½ cup dry white wine for the Chianti. Refrigerate or freeze the extra broth.

Homemade Beef or Lamb Broth

For a supply of homemade broth, proceed through Step 4 using beef or lamb shanks. Cool the remaining broth to room temperature, then refrigerate or freeze in 2-cup containers. (The broth can be stored for up to 3 days, covered in the refrigerator, or for up to 3 months in the freezer.) Makes about 2 quarts broth.

Makes 4 to 6 servings

ground beef and squash picadillo

Can Be Cooked in Under 30 Minutes

Coconut Rice or Steamed Rice (page 26), preferably made with medium-grain rice

1 medium (1½ pounds) acorn squash

Nonstick vegetable cooking spray

1½ pounds ground round

1 medium onion, chopped

1 medium green bell pepper, seeded and chopped

2 garlic cloves, minced

1½ cups Homemade Beef Broth (page 91) or low-sodium canned broth

¼ cup dark rum

2 tablespoons tomato paste

⅓ cup raisins

⅓ cup small pimiento-stuffed green olives

1 teaspoon cumin seeds, toasted and crushed (see page 124)

1 teaspoon dried oregano

¾ teaspoon salt

¼ teaspoon freshly ground black pepper

Picadillo is an all-purpose meat filling found all over Mexico and South America. While most local cooks would use calabaza, a pumpkinlike squash, I substitute the readily available acorn squash. My version gets a Caribbean note with a splash of dark rum.

1. Using a sharp knife, cut the acorn squash in half and scoop out the seeds with a large spoon. Cut the squash into 1-inch pieces. Using a small, sharp knife or a swivel-bladed vegetable peeler, pare off the skin. Set aside.

2. Spray a large (12-inch) nonstick skillet with nonstick cooking spray. Add the ground beef, onion, bell pepper, and garlic. Cook over medium-high heat, stirring often to break up the meat with a spoon, until the vegetables are softened, about 6 minutes. Tilt the pan to pour off excess fat.

3. Add the beef broth, rum, and tomato paste, and bring to a boil, stirring to dissolve the tomato paste. Add the raisins, olives, cumin, oregano, salt, and pepper. Arrange the squash on top. Reduce the heat to medium-low. Cover and simmer until the squash is tender, 15 to 20 minutes.

4. Spoon the rice into individual soup bowls. Top with the picadillo and serve immediately.

Makes 4 to 6 servings

mongolian lamb with broccoli

Can Be Cooked in Under 30 Minutes

*Steamed Rice (page 26), preferably
made with long-grain rice*

4 tablespoons soy sauce

4 tablespoons Scotch whisky

1 tablespoon plus 1 teaspoon
   cornstarch

1 tablespoon plus 2 teaspoons
   Asian dark sesame oil

1½ pounds lean lamb, cut into
   strips 2 inches long and
   ½ inch wide

½ cup Homemade Chicken
   Broth (page 75) or low-sodium
   canned broth

½ teaspoon Szechuan
   peppercorns, crushed

1½ pounds broccoli,
   trimmed into florets, stems cut
   into ¼-inch-thick slices

2 tablespoons vegetable oil,
   or more as needed

1 tablespoon minced fresh ginger

6 small dried chiles,
   such as japonés

3 garlic cloves, minced

2 bunches scallions, green and
   white parts, cut into 1-inch pieces

broccoli is just the right vegetable to stand up to lamb in this full-flavored stir-fry. If you have a good butcher nearby, ask him to cut thinly sliced lean lamb for stir-frying. Otherwise, cut the strips yourself, slicing across the grain, from trimmed leg of lamb steaks or round bone shoulder chops; buy a bit extra to allow for waste.

1. In a medium bowl, combine 2 tablespoons of the soy sauce, 2 tablespoons of the Scotch, 1 tablespoon of the cornstarch and 2 teaspoons of the sesame oil and whisk to dissolve the cornstarch. Add the lamb and toss. Let stand for 15 to 30 minutes.

2. In a small bowl, combine the remaining 2 tablespoons soy sauce, the remaining 2 tablespoons Scotch, the remaining 1 teaspoon cornstarch, and the remaining 1 tablespoon sesame oil, with the broth and Szechuan peppercorns. Whisk to dissolve the cornstarch. Set the broth mixture aside.

3. In a large (12-inch) nonstick skillet or wok, bring ½ cup water to a boil. Add the broccoli florets and stems and cover tightly. Cook until the broccoli is crisp-tender, about 3 minutes. Drain, rinse under cold water, and set aside. Wipe the skillet dry with paper towels.

4. Place the skillet over high heat until very hot. Add 1 tablespoon of the vegetable oil, tilting the pan to coat the bottom with the oil, and heat the oil until very hot. In 2 batches, using more oil as needed, cook the lamb, stirring occasionally, until the lamb is browned, about 4 minutes. Transfer to a plate and set aside.

5. Add the remaining 1 tablespoon oil to the skillet and heat until very hot. Add the ginger, chiles, and garlic and stir-fry until very fragrant, about 30 seconds. Add the scallions and stir-fry until bright green, about 1 minute. Return the lamb and broccoli to the skillet. Stir the broth mixture, add to the skillet, and cook until the sauce thickens, about 1 minute.

6. Spoon the rice into individual soup bowls and top with the lamb, vegetables, and sauce. Serve immediately.

Makes 4 to 6 servings

middle eastern lamb sauce with pine nuts and currants

Can Be Cooked in Under 30 Minutes

Steamed Rice (page 26), preferably made with basmati rice

½ cup (2 ounces) pine nuts

1 tablespoon olive oil

1 medium onion, chopped

2 medium (1 pound) zucchini, scrubbed and cut into ½-inch cubes

2 medium carrots, cut into ½-inch cubes

2 large garlic cloves, minced

1½ pounds lean ground lamb (see Note)

¾ cup Homemade Beef or Lamb Broth (page 91), or low-sodium canned beef broth

⅓ cup dried currants or raisins

2 tablespoons tomato paste

1 teaspoon dried oregano

¼ teaspoon ground allspice

¾ teaspoon salt

¼ teaspoon freshly ground black pepper

Most Americans, unfortunately, aren't familiar with the ancient cuisines of the Middle East, which often feature a blend of sweet and savory flavors, as in this delectable sauce. It has an intriguing mix of textures and tastes, including the warm scent of allspice and the crunch of pine nuts.

1. Heat a large (12-inch) nonstick skillet over medium heat. Add the pine nuts and cook, stirring almost constantly, until lightly toasted, about 2 minutes. Transfer to a plate and set aside.

2. Add the oil to the skillet and heat. Add the onion, zucchini, and carrots. Cook, stirring often, until the onion is golden, about 6 minutes. Add the garlic and cook for 1 minute. Add the lamb and increase the heat to medium-high. Cook, breaking up the lamb with a spoon, until it loses its pink color, about 6 minutes. Tilt the pan to pour off excess fat.

3. Add the broth, currants, tomato paste, oregano, and allspice, stirring to dissolve the tomato paste. Reduce the heat to low and simmer, uncovered, until the liquid almost completely reduces, but the meat sauce is still moist, about 10 minutes. Stir in the pine nuts. Season with the salt and pepper.

4. Spoon the rice into individual soup bowls, top with the lamb sauce and serve immediately.

Note: There is no USDA standard for ground lamb, so beware of fatty ground lamb. To control the amount of fat, ask the butcher to grind trimmed leg of lamb, not shoulder, which can be very fatty, for you. The meat should include about 10 percent visible fat, however, or it will be dry after cooking. You may also grind the meat yourself at home. Partially freeze cubes of trimmed lamb until semi-solid. Grind the lamb in a meat grinder or process in a food processor fitted with the metal blade until very finely chopped.

Makes 4 to 6 servings

lamb chops with zuni vegetable sauce

Herbed Rice with parsley or Steamed Rice (page 26), preferably made with long-grain rice

1 pound fresh tomatillos, husked, or 1 can (13 ounces) tomatillos, drained, rinsed, and crushed

1 tablespoon vegetable oil, or more as needed

6 shoulder lamb chops (8 ounces each)

Salt

Freshly ground black pepper

1 medium onion, chopped

2 medium (1 pound) yellow summer squash, chopped

1 medium red bell pepper, seeded and chopped

1 fresh chile, such as jalapeño, seeded and minced

2 large garlic cloves, minced

1 teaspoon cumin seed, toasted and crushed (see page 124)

1 teaspoon coriander seed, crushed

⅓ cup Homemade Beef or Lamb Broth (page 91), or low-sodium canned beef broth

1 cup fresh or frozen corn kernels

Native American foods—peppers, squash, and corn—combine to make a simple sauce for braised lamb chops. Fresh tomatillos, husk-covered fruits that resemble small green tomatoes, are available in season at Mexican or Central American markets and some supermarkets. Substitute canned tomatillos if the fresh are not available.

1. Bring salted water to a boil in a medium saucepan, add the tomatillos, and simmer just until tender, about 10 minutes. Be careful not to boil the tomatillos, or they may burst. Drain, rinse under cold water, and chop coarsely. Set aside.

2. In a large (12-inch) nonstick skillet, heat the oil over medium-high heat. In 2 batches, adding more oil as needed, add the lamb and cook, turning once, until browned on both sides, about 5 minutes. Transfer to a plate and season with ¼ teaspoon salt and ¼ teaspoon pepper. Set aside.

3. Add the onion, yellow squash, bell pepper, chile, and garlic to the skillet and reduce the heat to medium. Cook, stirring often, until the vegetables soften, about 8 minutes. Add the cumin and coriander and cook for 1 minute. Stir in the tomatillos and broth. Bring to a simmer and reduce the heat to low. Return the lamb chops to the skillet. Cover and simmer until the lamb and vegetables are tender, about 20 minutes. Transfer the lamb to a plate and cover to keep warm. Stir the corn into the sauce and cook for 2 minutes. Season with salt and pepper to taste.

4. Spoon the rice onto individual dinner plates. Top with the vegetable stew, and then place the lamb chops off to one side. Serve immediately.

Makes 4 to 6 servings

pork tenderloin with curried fruit sauce

Can Be Cooked in Under 30 Minutes

*Indian Spiced Rice, Coconut Rice,
or Steamed Rice (page 26),
preferably made with basmati rice*

¼ cup all-purpose flour

Salt

Freshly ground black pepper

1½ pounds boneless pork
tenderloin, cut crosswise into
¼-inch-thick medallions

2 tablespoons vegetable oil,
or more as needed

1 tart apple, peeled and chopped

1 medium onion, chopped

2 garlic cloves, minced

1½ teaspoons Madras
curry powder

1½ cups Homemade Chicken Broth
(page 75) or low-sodium canned
broth

1 ripe banana, finely chopped

⅓ cup plain yogurt

¼ teaspoon cornstarch

⅓ cup raisins

Chopped scallions, for garnish

Mango chutney, for serving

With apples or bananas in the fruit bowl and pork tenderloin in the freezer, this will become one of your favorite recipes to make when you don't feel like going to the grocery store.

1. In a shallow dish, mix the flour, ½ teaspoon salt, and ¼ teaspoon pepper. Coat both sides of the pork with the flour mixture, shaking off the excess. In a large (12-inch) nonstick skillet over medium-high heat, heat 1 tablespoon of the oil. In 2 batches add the pork and cook, turning once, until lightly browned, about 5 minutes. Add more oil as needed. Transfer to a plate and set aside.

2. Add the remaining 1 tablespoon oil to the skillet. Add the apple and onion and cover. Cook until the onion is golden, about 5 minutes. Stir in the garlic and cook, uncovered, for 1 minute. Add the curry powder and stir for 30 seconds.

3. Stir in the chicken broth and banana. Return the pork to the skillet and bring to a simmer. Reduce the heat to low and cook until the apple is tender and the sauce has thickened, about 3 minutes.

4. In a small bowl, stir together the yogurt and cornstarch until the cornstarch is dissolved. Add to the skillet, along with the raisins. Heat through gently, but do not boil. Season with salt and pepper to taste.

5. Spoon the rice onto dinner plates and top with the pork and sauce. Sprinkle with the scallions and serve immediately. Pass a bowl of chutney on the side.

Makes 4 to 6 servings

pork and mushroom goulash

Can Be Cooked in Under 30 Minutes

Steamed Rice (page 26), preferably made with long-grain rice

1 tablespoon oil

1½ pounds boneless pork loin, cut into ¾-inch cubes

1 medium onion, chopped

1 medium Italian frying or cubanella pepper, seeded and chopped

10 ounces mushrooms, halved

1 large garlic clove, minced

2 tablespoons all-purpose flour

1½ teaspoons sweet Hungarian paprika

1 teaspoon caraway seed, crushed

¼ teaspoon dried marjoram

1¾ cups Homemade Beef Broth (page 91) or low-sodium canned broth

¼ teaspoon salt

¼ teaspoon freshly ground black pepper

Sour cream, for garnish

Chile peppers are loved worldwide, and Hungarians are right up there with the Mexican and Cajun hotheads in their pursuit of the perfect capsicum, which flavors many of their favorite dishes. This quick skillet dish is related to a fine Hungarian goulash, so be sure to use the best Hungarian paprika. High-quality Hungarian paprika (both the versatile sweet as well as hot kinds) is now available at most supermarkets, and it is much better than a bland, inexpensive paprika that is fit only for sprinkling on top of casseroles. I prefer Italian frying or cubanella peppers in this dish; they have a more complex flavor than green bell peppers. If Italian or cubanella peppers are impossible to find, use the green peppers.

1. In a large (12-inch) nonstick skillet, heat the oil over medium-high heat. Add the pork and cook, turning occasionally, until browned, about 6 minutes. Transfer to a plate.

2. Add the onion, pepper, and mushrooms to the skillet. Cook, stirring often, until the mushrooms give off their liquid and it almost completely evaporates, about 6 minutes. Add the garlic and cook for 1 minute.

3. Sprinkle the vegetables with the flour, paprika, caraway seed, and marjoram and reduce the heat to medium. Stir until all of the ingredients are well coated, about 1 minute. Stir in the broth and bring to a simmer. Return the pork to the skillet. Reduce the heat to low and simmer, uncovered, until the pork is tender, about 20 minutes. Season with salt and pepper to taste.

4. Spoon the rice onto individual dinner plates, top with the goulash, and add a dollop of sour cream on each serving. Serve immediately.

Makes 4 to 6 servings

smoked pork chops with beer-braised cabbage

Steamed Rice (page 26), preferably made with long-grain rice, or Steamed Brown Rice (page 28)

Nonstick vegetable oil cooking spray

6 smoked pork loin chops, ¾-inch thick, bone in

1 tablespoon vegetable oil

1 large onion, chopped

2 medium carrots, cut into ½-inch-thick rounds

2 medium tart apples, such as Granny Smith, peeled, cored, and chopped into ¾-inch pieces

1 garlic clove, minced

1 small head (1½ pounds) Savoy cabbage, cored and thinly sliced (about 8 packed cups)

1 bottle (12 ounces) amber or lager beer

1 tablespoon light brown sugar

1 teaspoon caraway seed, crushed

¾ teaspoon salt

¼ teaspoon freshly ground black pepper

1 tablespoon Dijon mustard

1 tablespoon cider vinegar

1 tablespoon all-purpose flour

this hearty dish is emblematic of Old World cooking. Smoked pork loin chops appear only occasionally at the supermarket, but a good butcher, especially of Eastern European heritage, will be able to get them for you anytime. You could make this with unsmoked chops, too.

1. Spray a large (12-inch) nonstick skillet with vegetable oil spray and heat over medium-high heat. In batches, add the pork chops and cook, turning once, until lightly browned on both sides, about 5 minutes. Transfer to a plate and set aside.

2. Add the oil to the skillet and heat over medium heat. Add the onion, carrots, and apples. Cook, stirring often, until the onion is lightly browned, about 8 minutes. Add the garlic and cook for 1 minute. In 2 or 3 batches, stir in the cabbage, covering the skillet and letting the cabbage wilt before adding another batch.

3. Add the beer, brown sugar, caraway seed, salt, and pepper and bring to a simmer. Bury the pork chops in the cabbage.

Reduce the heat to medium-low and cover. Simmer until the cabbage is very tender, about 20 minutes. Transfer the pork chops to a plate and cover with foil to keep warm.

4. In a small bowl, combine the mustard, vinegar, and flour. Stir in ⅓ cup of the cooking liquid to make a thin paste. Stir the paste into the skillet and simmer until the cooking juices are thickened, about 2 minutes.

5. Spoon the rice onto individual dinner plates. Top each serving with cabbage and a pork chop and serve immediately.

Makes 4 to 6 servings

pork fajita stir-fry

Can Be Cooked in Under 30 Minutes

Beer Rice or Steamed Rice (page 28)

3 tablespoons fresh lime juice

2 tablespoons Worcestershire sauce

4 tablespoons olive oil, or more
as needed

1 tablespoon chili powder

1 teaspoon dried oregano

1 teaspoon cumin seed, toasted and
crushed (page 124)

1½ pounds boneless pork loin,
cut into strips 2 inches long and
½ inch wide

1 onion, cut into ¼-inch-thick
half moons

1 large red bell pepper, seeded and
cut into ½-inch-wide strips

1 large green bell pepper, seeded
and cut into ½-inch-wide strips

2 garlic cloves, minced

½ cup Homemade Beef
Broth (page 91), or low-sodium
canned broth

2 tablespoons tomato paste

¼ teaspoon salt

¼ teaspoon freshly ground
black pepper

Chopped cilantro, for garnish

Sour cream and chopped ripe
avocados, for garnish (optional)

tortilla-wrapped fajitas are fun, but they can be a bit fussy, not to mention sloppy to eat. When you just can't deal with all that stuffing and rolling, make this pork stir-fry. The meat is marinated in a terrific lime-chile soak and sautéed with plenty of sweet peppers. Try to remember to marinate the pork early in the day. My trick is to prepare the marinade in a heavy-duty zipper-type plastic bag the night before and refrigerate it until the next morning. Then, just before leaving the house, I quickly add the meat to the bag, and let the meat and marinade get to know each other in the refrigerator while I'm out all day.

1. In a large plastic storage bag, mix the lime juice, Worcestershire sauce, 2 tablespoons of the oil, chili powder, oregano, and cumin. Add the pork strips and toss. Cover with plastic wrap and refrigerate, at least 1 hour and up to 8 hours.

2. Heat a large (12-inch) nonstick skillet over medium-high heat. Add 1 tablespoon of the remaining oil and tilt the skillet to coat the bottom. Add the onion, red pepper, and green pepper. Stir-fry until the vegetables are crisp-tender, about 3 minutes. Add the garlic and cook for 1 minute. Transfer to a bowl and set aside.

3. Remove the pork from the marinade, pouring the marinade into a bowl. Stir the beef broth and tomato paste into the marinade and set aside.

4. Heat the remaining 1 tablespoon oil in the skillet over medium-high heat. In 2 batches, cook the pork strips, adding more oil as needed, stirring often, until the pork is browned, about 4 minutes.

5. Return the pork and peppers to the skillet. Add the broth mixture and cook until the sauce is slightly reduced, about 3 minutes. Season with the salt and pepper.

6. Spoon the rice into individual serving bowls, top with the pork stir-fry, and sprinkle with the cilantro. Serve immediately. Pass bowls of avocado and sour cream on the side, if desired.

Makes 4 to 6 servings

new york diner fried rice

Can Be Cooked in Under 30 Minutes

1 tablespoon vegetable oil

6 ounces chorizo or other spicy smoked sausage, such as linguiça, andouille, or kielbasa, cut into ½-inch pieces

1 medium onion, chopped

1 medium green bell pepper, seeded and chopped

1 garlic clove, minced

1 teaspoon chili powder

1 teaspoon dried oregano

3 cups chilled cooked rice, rubbed between your fingers to separate the grains

2 medium tomatoes, seeded and chopped

½ teaspoon salt

2 large eggs, beaten

ere's a recipe for leftover rice. Asian-owned diners that serve Central American dishes are found all over Manhattan. Their storefronts announce *Comidas Chinas* (Spanish for Chinese food), but they actually sell both kinds, including some delicious hybrids like this quick supper dish. Be sure to use chilled cooked rice, as warm rice will clump.

1. In a large (12-inch) nonstick skillet, heat the oil over medium heat. Add the chorizo and cook, stirring occasionally, until lightly browned, about 5 minutes.

2. Add the onion, bell pepper, and garlic. Cook, stirring often, until the onion is softened, about 5 minutes. Stir in the chili powder and oregano.

3. Add the rice and cook, stirring often, until the rice is heated through, about 3 minutes. Stir in the tomatoes and salt.

4. Make a well in the center of the rice. Pour in the eggs and stir the eggs until partially set and creamy, about 30 seconds. Mix thoroughly into the rice and cook until the egg is set, about 1 minute.

5. Spoon the fried rice into individual soup bowls and serve immediately.

Makes 4 to 6 servings

cauliflower and carrot curry

szechuan spicy eggplant

green beans and red pepper with black bean sauce

lentil and swiss chard stew

rosario's mushroom-vegetable chili

spinach and chick peas in spiced yogurt

quick fresh tomato and basil sauce

greek tomato sauce with marinated artichokes and feta cheese

gazpacho rice salad ring

summer vegetable fricassee

vegetable ragout, provençale style

sushi rice bowl

moroccan tagine

spanish artichoke and asparagus stew

old-fashioned vegetable-rice soup

mixed venetian vegetable stew

roasted vegetables in orange teriyaki

FROM THE garden

it

wasn't too long ago that people were divided into two culinary camps—vegetarians and meat eaters, like teetotalers and martini-drinkers. There wasn't much middle ground.

The old stereotype of the virtuous vegetarian (wearing tie-dyed clothes with sensible sandals and carrying an animal rights placard) has disappeared. More and more people are turning to meatless meals simply because they enjoy them for their healthfulness and flavor. Another reason for the vegetable victory is that better produce is becoming available with each passing day. Many supermarkets now carry organic produce, and large natural food stores with a commitment to sustainable agriculture are springing up all over the country, as are local small farmers' markets that showcase seasonal food at its peak.

While many vegetable stir-fries and sauces cook quickly, some are stews that need to simmer for a while for the flavors to blend. In my opinion, barely cooked vegetables are highly overrated. When the vegetables are young, sweet, and freshly picked, they can be delicious served crisp-tender. However, in a dish like the Spanish Artichoke and Asparagus Stew, the vegetables should be well cooked. Bitter greens, as in the Salmon Fillets on Broccoli Rabe (page 46), need to be cooked until the bitterness is reduced, at least 30 minutes.

It is imperative to use a good vegetable broth in meatless cooking. There are canned vegetable broths and vegetable bouillon cubes available, but taste them first to be sure they are up to your standards. I was thrilled to find canned vegetable broth at the supermarket, but not so happy when I actually tasted it, since I don't necessarily want beet juice in every dish I make. It is easy to strain the vegetables from the Old-Fashioned Vegetable-Rice Soup, and use the broth in your recipes. Unless you are going one hundred percent vegetarian, all of these recipes will work with chicken broth, too.

Fresh vegetables are supposed to be best, but American shoppers have gotten into the habit of demanding out-of-season produce year round, so fresh does not always mean tasty. For cooking out of season, some vegetables are more reliable frozen or canned. Keep bags of peas and corn in the freezer and rinse them in a sieve under hot water for a quick thawing. Canned tomatoes come in many forms— in juice, in tomato puree, and crushed. Imported Italian tomatoes are best, preferably San Marzano, but they can be pricey. Try a few different brands of canned tomatoes and choose the one that has the firmest unblemished tomatoes and the thickest tomato juice.

cauliflower and carrot curry

Can Be Cooked in Under 30 Minutes

Steamed Rice (page 26), preferably made with basmati rice

1 tablespoon vegetable oil

4 large carrots, cut into ½-inch rounds

1 medium onion, chopped

2 garlic cloves, minced

1 tablespoon Madras curry powder

1 teaspoon cumin seed, toasted and crushed (see page 124)

1 medium head (2 pounds) cauliflower, cut into small florets

1 cup Homemade Vegetable Broth (page 126), vegetable bouillon, or canned broth

½ cup canned unsweetened coconut milk (see page 54)

1 cup thawed frozen peas

¼ teaspoon salt

here's a colorful vegetarian curry that is easy to make. Ripe summer vegetables get a lot of press, but I enjoy the challenge of making something tasty out of the inexpensive, plebeian vegetables that are available year round.

1. In a dutch oven or flameproof casserole, heat the oil over medium heat. Add the carrots and onion. Cook, stirring often, until the onions are golden, about 6 minutes. Stir in the garlic and cook for 1 minute. Add the curry and cumin and stir for 30 seconds.

2. Add the cauliflower, vegetable broth, and coconut milk. Bring to a boil and reduce the heat to low. Cover and simmer until the vegetables are tender, 10 to 15 minutes. Add the peas and cook until heated through, about 2 minutes. Season with the salt.

3. Spoon the rice into individual soup bowls and top with the curry. Serve immediately.

Makes 4 to 6 servings

szechuan spicy eggplant

Can Be Cooked in Under 30 Minutes

Steamed Rice (page 26), preferably made with long-grain rice

3 pounds (2 to 3 large Mediterranean or 12 small Asian) eggplant, cut into ¾-inch pieces

Salt

1½ tablespoons vegetable oil

1½ tablespoons minced fresh ginger

5 scallions, green and white parts, finely chopped

5 garlic cloves, minced

2 cups Homemade Vegetable Broth (page 126), vegetable bouillon, or canned broth

3 tablespoons soy sauce

1½ tablespoon rice vinegar

1 tablespoon Asian dark sesame oil

1 tablespoon sugar

1 teaspoon Chinese chile paste with garlic (see Note) or ½ teaspoon crushed red pepper

Sesame seeds, for garnish

this is an eggplant lover's dream. It can be made with both the familiar purple Mediterranean eggplant and the elongated lavender Asian variety—both work well, although the Asian variety has a mellower flavor and does not need to be salted.

1. If desired, place the eggplant in a colander and sprinkle with 2 teaspoons salt. Let stand for at least 20 minutes or up to l hour. Rinse well under cold water and pat completely dry with paper towels.

2. Heat a large (12-inch) nonstick skillet or wok over medium-high heat. Add the oil and heat until the oil is hot. Add the eggplant, ginger, scallions, and garlic. Stir-fry until well-mixed, about 1 minute.

3. Stir in the broth, soy sauce, vinegar, sesame oil, sugar, and chile paste and bring to a boil. Cook, stirring often, until the eggplant is very tender and the sauce is thickened, about 10 minutes. Season with additional salt, to taste.

4. Spoon the rice into individual soup bowls and top with the eggplant and sauce. Sprinkle with the sesame seeds and serve immediately.

Note: Chinese chile paste with garlic is available at Asian markets and by mail order (see page 140).

Makes 4 to 6 servings

green beans and red pepper with black bean sauce

Can Be Cooked in Under 30 Minutes

Steamed Rice (page 26), preferably made with long-grain rice

1 tablespoon vegetable oil

2 pounds green beans, trimmed and cut into 1-inch lengths

1 large red bell pepper, seeded and cut into ½-inch-wide strips

1 large onion, cut into ¼-inch-thick half moons

1 tablespoon minced fresh ginger

5 large garlic cloves, minced

¾ cup Homemade Vegetable Broth (page 126), or canned broth

2 tablespoons Chinese black bean sauce (see Note)

1 tablespoon soy sauce

2 tablespoons rice wine or dry vermouth

1 teaspoon sugar

¼ teaspoon crushed red pepper, or more to taste

1½ teaspoons cornstarch dissolved in ¼ cup water

In Chinese cooking, green beans are often deep-fried, then glazed with a rich sauce. I prefer to sauté the beans for a dish with the same flavors but much less fat, adding red bell pepper for a colorful accent.

1. Heat a large (12-inch) nonstick skillet or wok over medium-high heat. Add the oil and heat until very hot. Add the green beans, pepper strips, and onion. Cook, stirring often, until the vegetables are crisp-tender and some of the beans are tinged with brown spots, about 6 minutes.

2. Add the ginger and garlic and stir-fry for 1 minute. Add the broth, bean sauce, soy sauce, rice wine, sugar and crushed red pepper. Bring to a boil. Stir the cornstarch mixture, add to the skillet, and cook until the sauce is thickened, about 1 minute.

3. Spoon the rice into individual soup bowls and top with the vegetables and sauce. Serve immediately.

Note: Black bean sauce is available at Asian markets and by mail order (see page 140).

Variation

Green Beans with Pork in Garlic Sauce: Add 4 ounces ground pork to the vegetables in Step 1, breaking up the meat with a spoon as it cooks.

Makes 4 to 6 servings

lentil and swiss chard stew

Herbed Rice with parsley or Steamed Rice (page 26), preferably made with basmati rice

¼ pound Swiss chard, well rinsed

1 tablespoon olive oil

1 large onion, chopped

2 medium carrots, chopped

2 medium celery ribs
with leaves, chopped

2 garlic cloves, minced

8 ounces (1 generous cup)
dried lentils

3 cups Homemade Vegetable
Broth (page 126), vegetable
bouillon, or canned broth

¾ teaspoon dried rosemary

¾ teaspoon dried thyme

1 bay leaf

¼ teaspoon freshly ground
black pepper, or more as needed

1 cup dry white wine

2 tablespoons tomato paste

¾ teaspoon salt, or more as needed

O f all the dried legumes, lentils are the quickest to cook. They make it possible to create a hearty bean dish without the fuss of presoaking. Like many similar stews that include meat, this vegetarian version is well seasoned with wine and herbs.

1. Cut off the stems of the swiss chard leaves and cut crosswise into ½-inch-thick pieces. Set aside. Cut the leaves crosswise into ½-inch-wide strips. Set aside separately from the stems.

2. In a dutch oven or flameproof casserole, heat the oil over medium heat. Add the Swiss chard stems, onion, carrots, celery, and garlic. Cover and cook, stirring often, until the vegetables soften, about 5 minutes. Stir in the lentils.

3. Add the vegetable broth, rosemary, thyme, bay leaf, and pepper and bring to a boil. Reduce the heat to low and cover.

Simmer for 25 minutes. Stir in the wine, tomato paste, and salt. Cook, covered, until the lentils are tender, about 15 minutes. Stir in the swiss chard strips, cover, and cook until tender, about 5 minutes. Taste and season with additional salt and pepper as needed. Discard the bay leaf.

4. Spoon the rice into individual soup bowls and top with the lentil stew. Serve immediately.

Makes 4 to 6 servings

rosario's mushroom-vegetable chili

Beer Rice or Steamed Rice (page 26), preferably made with long-grain rice

3 tablespoons olive oil

3 ounces (about 9) ancho chiles, stemmed, seeded, and coarsely chopped (see Note)

6 garlic cloves, crushed

2 cups boiling water

1 medium onion, chopped

2 medium (about 1 pound) zucchini, cut into ½-inch pieces

2 pounds fresh mushrooms, sliced

1½ cups fresh or frozen corn kernels

1 teaspoon salt

Shredded monterey jack cheese, for serving

my friend Rosario, a talented sculptor who lives in Mexico, visits her American friends once a year, and when she does, we ask her to prepare her authentically heady vegetable chili, made with ancho chiles. Rosario usually makes it only with mushrooms, but I like to add other vegetables, too.

1. In a large (12-inch) nonstick skillet, heat the oil over low heat. Add the chiles and garlic. Cook slowly until the garlic is golden brown, about 5 minutes.

2. Using a slotted spoon, transfer the chilies and garlic to a bowl, leaving the oil in the skillet. Pour the boiling water into the bowl and let the chiles stand until softened, about 30 minutes. Set the skillet aside until ready to proceed.

3. Reheat the oil over medium heat. Add the onion and cook until softened, about 3 minutes. Add the zucchini and increase the heat to medium-high. Cook until lightly browned, about 8 minutes. Add the mushrooms and cook until the mushrooms give off their liquid, about 5 minutes.

4. Transfer the chiles and garlic with their soaking liquid to a blender and puree until they form a paste. Scrape the paste into the mushrooms and mix well. Bring to a simmer. Reduce the heat to low. Simmer, uncovered, stirring often, until the sauce has thickened, about 15 minutes. During the last 5 minutes of cooking, stir in the corn. Season with the salt.

5. Spoon the rice into individual soup bowls and top with the chili. Serve immediately. Pass a bowl of cheese for sprinkling.

Note: Dried New Mexican chiles, available at many supermarkets, can be substituted for the ancho chiles, although they are milder.

Variation

Rosario's Mushroom Chili with Chicken: During the last 5 minutes of cooking, stir in 2 cups cooked chicken cut into bite-size pieces.

Makes 4 to 6 servings

spinach and chick peas in spiced yogurt

Can Be Cooked in Under 30 Minutes

Indian Spiced Rice or Steamed Rice (page 26), preferably made with basmati rice

2 pounds tender fresh spinach, well rinsed

1 tablespoon vegetable oil

2 large onions, cut into ¼-inch-thick half moons

2 tablespoons minced fresh ginger

3 garlic cloves, minced

1 teaspoon Garam Masala (recipe follows)

1 can (15 ounces) chick peas, drained and rinsed

½ teaspoon salt, or more as needed

¼ teaspoon ground red pepper, or more as needed

1 cup plain lowfat yogurt

1 teaspoon cornstarch

reserve this recipe for young, tender spinach with delicate stems. If you must use supermarket packaged leaves, remove the stems and finely chop them. Gently seasoned with the Indian spice blend garam masala, this is usually served as a side dish, but its creamy character makes it a flawless vegetarian main course when served on rice. Garam masala, a blend of spices used in many Indian recipes, is available at Indian grocers. You can also make your own. It is best when made with freshly ground spices. A mini blender or electric coffee grinder works well.

1. Cut off the spinach leaves stems and cut them into ½-inch lengths. Set aside. Coarsely chop the spinach leaves. Set the leaves aside separately from the stems.

2. In a large (12-inch) nonstick skillet, heat the oil over medium-low heat. Add the onions and cover. Cook until the onions are very soft, about 10 minutes. Uncover and increase the heat to medium-high. Cook until the onions are golden brown, about 5 minutes. Add the ginger and garlic and cook for 1 minute.

3. Add the spinach stems and the Garam Masala. Stir until the stems are softened, about 1 minute. In batches, stir in the spinach leaves, allowing 1 batch to wilt before adding the next. Stir in the chick peas, salt, and hot pepper. Cover and cook until the spinach leaves are tender, about 5 minutes. Reduce the heat to low.

4. In a small bowl, stir together the yogurt and cornstarch. Pour into the skillet and stir until the yogurt is heated through, about 1 minute. Taste and season with more salt and hot pepper as needed.

5. Spoon the rice into individual soup bowls and top with the spinach, chick peas, and sauce. Serve immediately.

Garam Masala

Mix 1 teaspoon each ground cinnamon and ground cardamom; ½ teaspoon each ground cloves, ground cumin, and freshly ground black pepper, and ¼ teaspoon ground coriander. (Store, tightly covered, in a cool dry place.)

Makes 4 to 6 servings

quick fresh tomato and basil sauce

Can Be Cooked in Under 30 Minutes

Boiled Rice (page 27), preferably made with Italian rice

1½ tablespoons extra virgin olive oil

1 large onion, chopped

2 garlic cloves, minced

3 pounds ripe tomatoes, seeded and coarsely chopped

½ cup chopped basil

½ teaspoon salt

⅛ teaspoon crushed red pepper

Freshly grated Parmesan cheese, for serving

Quickly cooked, this sauce retains the tomatoes' fresh taste and texture. Just about any fine, summer harvest tomato will do—cherry tomatoes, plum tomatoes, huge beefsteaks, red, gold, or striped, or even a combination. But hold off until you get good ripe tomatoes!

1. In a large (12-inch) nonstick skillet, heat the oil over medium heat. Add the onion and cook until golden, about 5 minutes. Stir in the garlic and cook for 1 minute. Add the tomatoes and basil. Cook, stirring often, until the tomatoes soften and release their juices, about 5 minutes. Season with the salt and red pepper.

2. Spoon the rice into individual soup bowls and top with the tomato sauce. Serve immediately. Pass the Parmesan on the side.

Makes 4 to 6 servings

greek tomato sauce with marinated artichokes and feta cheese

Can Be Cooked in Under 30 Minutes

Mediterranean Pasta and Rice or Steamed Rice (page 26), preferably made with long-grain rice

2 jars (8 ounces each) marinated artichoke hearts

2 tablespoons reserved artichoke marinade

3 scallions, white and green parts, chopped

2 garlic cloves, minced

3 pounds ripe plum tomatoes, peeled, seeded, and coarsely chopped (page 54), or 2 cans (28 ounces each) Italian plum tomatoes, drained and coarsely chopped

½ cup (4 ounces) black Mediterranean olives, pitted and coarsely chopped

1½ teaspoons dried oregano

⅛ teaspoon ground cinnamon

¼ teaspoon crushed red pepper or freshly ground black pepper

Salt

6 ounces feta cheese, crumbled

Olives, feta cheese, marinated artichoke hearts—three ingredients that are almost always included in a Greek *meze* platter, served before the meal like the Italian antipasti. A hint of cinnamon adds another Greek touch to this easy tomato sauce. I prefer Bulgarian feta cheese to the other imported and domestic kinds. It is smoother and less salty with a milder tang.

1. Drain the artichokes, reserving 2 tablespoons of the marinade. Coarsely chop the artichokes and set aside.

2. In a large (12-ounce) nonstick skillet, heat the reserved marinade over medium heat. Add the scallions and garlic and cook, stirring often, until softened, about 2 minutes. Add the tomatoes, artichoke hearts, olives, oregano, cinnamon, and red pepper. Cook, stirring often, until the tomatoes soften and release their juices, about 6 minutes. Season with salt to taste, keeping in mind that the cheese topping will be salty.

3. Spoon the rice into individual soup bowls and top with the sauce. Sprinkle each serving with the cheese and serve immediately.

Makes 4 to 6 servings

gazpacho rice salad ring

Can Be Cooked in Under 30 Minutes

Dressing

2 tablespoons sherry vinegar

2 tablespoons fresh lemon juice

Grated zest of 1 lemon

1 garlic clove, crushed
  through a press

1 teaspoon sweet Hungarian paprika

1 teaspoon cumin seed, toasted
  and crushed (see page 124)

½ teaspoon dried oregano

½ teaspoon salt, or more
  as needed

¼ teaspoon crushed red pepper,
  or more as needed

¾ cup olive oil

1½ cups long-grain rice

1 large beefsteak tomato, seeded
  and chopped into ¾-inch pieces

2 Kirby (pickling) cucumbers,
  scrubbed and chopped into
  ½-inch pieces

1 small green bell pepper, seeded
  and chopped into ½-inch pieces

3 scallions, white and green
  parts, chopped

When you want a spectacular salad for a summer buffet, look no farther than this beauty. There are two caveats to rice salads. First, and very important to remember, is that rice hardens when chilled, so always serve rice salads at room temperature. Secondly, rice salads (like pasta salads) soak up dressing and need to be reseasoned if allowed to stand for long. If you must make the salad ahead of time, chill it in a bowl. About one hour before serving, reseason with lemon juice, oil, salt, and pepper, and pack into the mold. Let stand at room temperature, then unmold onto the serving platter.

1. To make the dressing, in a medium bowl, whisk together the vinegar, lemon juice, lemon zest, garlic, paprika, cumin, oregano, salt, and crushed red pepper. Gradually whisk in the oil. Set the dressing aside.

2. Bring a large pot of boiling salted water to a boil. Add the rice and cook until just tender, about 9 minutes. Drain, rinse under cold running water, and drain well. Place in a large bowl. (You will have about 4½ cups of rice.)

3. Add the tomato, cucumbers, bell pepper, and scallions and toss well. Add the dressing and toss again. Taste and season with salt and pepper as needed. Pack the salad into a lightly oiled 10-cup fluted tube mold or two 5- to 6-cup ring molds. Unmold the salad onto a serving platter and serve immediately.

Makes 4 to 6 servings

summer vegetable fricassee

Can Be Cooked in Under 30 Minutes

Steamed Rice (page 26), preferably made with popcorn rice

1½ tablespoons olive oil

1 large zucchini, cut into ½-inch cubes

1 medium red bell pepper, seeded and chopped

4 scallions, chopped

1 hot chile, such as jalapeño, seeded and finely chopped

2 large garlic cloves, minced

3½ cups fresh corn kernels (about 7 ears; see Note), or thawed frozen corn

1½ cups Homemade Vegetable Broth (page 126), vegetable bouillon, or canned broth

1½ cups reduced-fat sour cream

6 plum tomatoes, seeded and chopped

1 teaspoon ground toasted cumin seed (see page 124)

1½ tablespoons chopped oregano leaves

¼ teaspoon salt

¼ teaspoon freshly ground black pepper

Sprigs of cilantro or oregano, for garnish

my eyes are bigger than my shopping bag. I always buy too much produce at my farmers' market, especially in the summer. This creamy and spicy vegetable stew was inspired by one such shopping spree. While it can be made year round, the fresher the vegetables, the better the fricassee. If you like cilantro you can substitute 3 tablespoons for the oregano.

1. In a dutch oven or flameproof skillet, heat the oil over medium-high heat. Add the zucchini and red pepper. Cook, stirring occasionally, until lightly browned, about 5 minutes. Add the scallions, chile pepper, and garlic. Cover and cook, stirring often, until the vegetables soften, about 2 minutes.

2. Stir in the corn. Cook, uncovered, until the corn is heated through, stirring occasionally, about 2 minutes.

3. Add the broth, bring to a boil, and cook until slightly reduced, about 2 minutes. Add the sour cream, tomatoes, cumin, and oregano. Stir gently just until heated through, about 1 minute. Do not let the sour cream come to a boil or it may curdle. Season with salt and pepper.

4. Spoon the cooked rice into individual soup bowls and top with the fricassee. Garnish with the cilantro or oregano sprigs and serve immediately.

Note: To remove corn kernels from ears, trim off the ends of a husked ear. Stand the ear up on a cut end, and hold securely. Using a sharp knife, cut down where the kernels are attached to the ear, continuing until all of the kernels are cut off. Each ear will yield about ½ cup kernels.

Makes 4 to 6 servings

vegetable ragout, provençale style

*French Rice or Steamed Rice
(page 26), preferably made with
long-grain rice*

1 pound eggplant, peeled and
   cut into ¾-inch pieces

Salt

2 tablespoons extra virgin olive oil

1 medium onion, chopped

1 medium red bell pepper, seeded
   and cut into ½-inch pieces

1 medium zucchini, scrubbed and
   cut into ½-inch pieces

2 medium celery rib, cut into
   ¼-inch-thick slices

2 medium carrots, cut into
   ¼-inch-thick rounds

1½ teaspoons Herbes de
   Provence (recipe follows)

2 large garlic cloves, minced

2 cups tomato sauce

½ cup red wine

¼ teaspoon crushed red pepper

1 cup (8 ounces) green olives,
   pitted and coarsely chopped

Chopped basil or parsley, for garnish

this zesty stew is a relative of ratatouille, the long-simmered vegetable mélange that graces many a table in the south of France. Red wine adds a nontraditional, but welcome, fillip. Herbes de Provence is a mixture of dried herbs. You can find it at specialty food stores, or make your own.

1. If desired, place the eggplant in a colander and sprinkle with 1½ teaspoons salt. Let stand for at least 20 minutes or up to 1 hour. Rinse well under cold water and pat completely dry with paper towels.

2. In a large dutch oven or flameproof casserole, heat the oil over medium-high heat. Add the eggplant, onion, bell pepper, zucchini, celery, carrots, Herbes de Provence. Cook, stirring often, until the onion softens, about 3 minutes. Reduce the heat to medium and cover tightly. Cook until the eggplant is tender, about 8 minutes. Stir in the garlic and cook for 1 minute.

3. Stir in the tomato sauce, red wine and red pepper. Bring to a simmer. Reduce the heat to medium-low and simmer, stirring, until all of the vegetables are tender, about 15 minutes. During the last 5 minutes of cooking, stir in the olives. Season with additional salt to taste.

4. Spoon the rice into individual soup bowls and top with the ragout. Serve immediately, sprinkled with the basil.

Herbes de Provence

Mix together 1 teaspoon each dried basil, oregano, thyme, and savory with ½ teaspoon dried lavender. (Store, tightly covered, in a cool dry place.)

Makes 4 to 6 servings

sushi rice bowl

Can Be Cooked in Under 30 Minutes

Steamed Rice (page 26), preferably made with sushi rice

8 ounces snow peas, trimmed and halved crosswise

Nonstick vegetable cooking spray

2 large eggs

Pinch of salt

Pinch of freshly ground pepper

2 teaspoons vegetable oil

10 ounces shiitake mushrooms, stems removed, caps cut into ¼-inch-wide strips, or button mushrooms, stems and caps sliced ¼-inch-thick.

2 medium carrots, cut into thin sticks 2 inches long and ¼-inch-wide

1 cup Homemade Vegetable Broth (page 126), vegetable bouillon, or canned broth

2 tablespoons soy sauce

2 tablespoons dry sherry

2 tablespoons rice vinegar

1 tablespoon sugar

2 cups (6 ounces) bean sprouts

2 teaspoons cornstarch dissolved in 2 tablespoons water

Chopped scallions, for garnish

One of my favorite things to order at a Japanese sushi restaurant is *chirashi-zushi,* a mixture of vegetables arranged over cooled vinegar-and-sugar seasoned rice. When I want a quick home-cooked meal and am too impatient to cool the rice, I mix up all of the ingredients and serve them hot. In order to save a pot, remove the snow peas from their cooking water with a slotted spoon and use their water to prepare the rice.

1. In a medium saucepan of boiling salted water over high heat, cook the snow peas just until bright green, about 30 seconds. Drain, rinse under cold running water, and set aside.

2. Spray a large (12-inch) nonstick skillet or wok with nonstick cooking spray and heat over medium heat. In a small bowl, beat the eggs with the salt and pepper until very well mixed. Pour into the skillet, tilting the skillet to coat the bottom with the eggs. Reduce the heat to low and cook until the egg is set, about 2 minutes. Remove the skillet from the heat.

3. Using a rubber spatula, loosen the edges of the egg pancake. Still in the pan, roll up the egg pancake into a cylinder. Slide out of the pan onto a work surface and cool slightly. Cut crosswise into ¼-inch-wide strips. Unroll the strips and set aside.

4. Add the oil to the skillet and increase the heat to medium-high. Add the mushrooms and carrots. Cook until the mushrooms are lightly browned, about 4 minutes. Add the broth, soy sauce, sherry, vinegar, and sugar and bring to a simmer. Add the bean sprouts. Stir the cornstarch mixture, add to the skillet, and cook until the sauce is lightly thickened, about 1 minute. Stir in the snow peas.

5. Spoon the rice into individual soup bowls. Top with the vegetables and then the egg strips. Sprinkle with the scallions and serve immediately.

Makes 4 to 6 servings

moroccan tagine

Can Be Cooked in Under 30 Minutes

Steamed Rice (page 26), preferably made with basmati rice

1 (1½ pounds) acorn squash

2 tablespoons olive oil

1 medium onion, chopped

2 carrots, cut into ½-inch pieces

1 cup Homemade Vegetable Broth (page 126), vegetable bouillon, or canned broth

2 medium (1 pound) zucchini, scrubbed and cut into ½-inch-thick rounds

2 garlic cloves, minced

1 teaspoon sweet Hungarian paprika

1 teaspoon toasted ground cumin (see Note)

¼ teaspoon ground allspice

¼ teaspoon ground hot pepper

1 can (16 ounces) plum tomatoes, drained and chopped

1 can (15 ounces) chick peas, drained and rinsed

2 tablespoons fresh lemon juice

1 teaspoon sugar

⅓ cup raisins

Chopped cilantro, for garnish

Moroccans use couscous as their main starch, but there is no reason that their famous stewlike tagines couldn't be served on rice, too. This well-seasoned stew, tangy with lemon juice and lightly sweetened with raisins, is an excellent choice for a hearty, warming vegetarian meal on a cold evening.

1. Using a sharp knife, cut the acorn squash in half and scoop out the seeds with a large spoon. Cut the squash into 1-inch pieces. Using a small, sharp knife or a swivel-bladed vegetable peeler, pare off the skin. Set the squash aside.

2. In a large dutch oven or flameproof casserole, heat the oil over medium heat. Add the onion and cook until golden, about 5 minutes. Add the squash, carrots, and ½ cup of the broth. Cover tightly and reduce the heat to medium-low. Cook until the squash is almost tender, about 6 minutes.

3. Add the zucchini, garlic, paprika, cumin, allspice, and hot pepper. Cook, uncovered, stirring often, until the broth is almost evaporated, about 5 minutes.

4. Add the remaining ½ cup broth, the tomatoes, chick peas, lemon juice, and sugar, and bring to a simmer. Cook, stirring often, until the vegetables are tender, about 10 minutes. During the last 5 minutes, stir in the raisins.

5. Spoon the rice into individual soup bowls and top with the tagine. Sprinkle with the cilantro and serve immediately.

Note: To prepare the cumin, toast the seeds in a medium skillet, stirring often, until fragrant, 2 to 3 minutes. Transfer to a mortar and crush coarsely. The seeds can also be placed on a work surface and crushed underneath a heavy skillet or pot, or ground in an electric spice or coffee grinder. Two teaspoons of cumin seeds yield 1 teaspoon ground cumin.

Makes 4 to 6 servings

spanish artichoke and asparagus stew

Steamed Rice (page 26), preferably
made with medium-grain rice

2 tablespoons vinegar

3 medium artichokes, preferably
with stems attached

3 tablespoons olive oil

3 medium leeks, white parts only,
chopped (1 cup)

2 garlic cloves, minced

1 can (16 ounces) plum tomatoes,
drained and chopped

1 teaspoon cumin seeds, toasted
and crushed (see page 124)

½ teaspoon ground coriander

½ teaspoon sweet paprika

Salt

¼ teaspoon crushed red pepper

1½ cups Homemade Vegetable
Broth (page 126), vegetable
bouillon, or canned broth

⅓ cup dry sherry

1 pound asparagus, trimmed, cut
into 1-inch lengths

¾ pound green beans, trimmed,
cut into 1-inch lengths

¼ teaspoon saffron threads,
crushed (optional)

6 large eggs

Freshly ground black pepper

during a leisurely trip through Spain, I enjoyed many savory vegetable stews created from just-picked produce. Long simmered, the vegetables were never crisp, but the flavors were beautifully mingled. The fried egg is an imperative finishing touch, adding a subtle enrichment to the stew's juices.

1. In a medium bowl, stir the vinegar into 4 cups of water. Working with 1 artichoke at a time, snap back the hard outer leaves to reveal the inner core of tender light green leaves. About 1 inch above where they meet the indentation of the solid artichoke base, cut off the tops of the leaves. Dip the artichoke in the vinegar water. Using a small sharp knife, pare away the dark green skin from the stem and artichoke bottom. Cut the artichoke bottom into quarters. Using the tip of the knife, dig out the fuzzy choke from the center of each quarter. Drop the quarters into the water.

2. In a large dutch oven or flameproof casserole, heat 1 tablespoon of the oil over medium-low heat. Add the leeks and garlic and cover. Cook until the leeks are softened, about 5 minutes. Stir in the tomatoes, cumin, coriander, paprika, 1 teaspoon salt, and red pepper. Increase the heat to medium-high. Cook, stirring often, until the tomato liquid is almost completely evaporated, about 4 minutes.

3. Stir in the broth and sherry and bring to a boil. Drain the artichoke quarters and add to the sauce. Cover and reduce the heat to medium-low. Simmer until the artichokes are almost tender, about 20 minutes. Stir in the asparagus and green beans and continue to cook, covered, until all the vegetables are very tender, about 20 minutes. During the last 5 minutes, stir in the saffron, if using.

4. In a large (12-inch) nonstick skillet, heat the remaining 2 tablespoons oil over medium heat. One at a time, gently break the eggs into the skillet. Cover and cook until the edges of the eggs are set, about 1 minute. Carefully turn the eggs and cook just until the yolks are set but still runny, about 1 minute. Season the eggs with salt and black pepper to taste.

5. Spoon the rice into individual soup bowls. Top each serving with the vegetable stew and then an egg. Serve immediately.

Makes 4 to 6 servings

old-fashioned vegetable-rice soup

*Boiled Rice (page 27), made
with 1 cup long-grain rice*

Vegetable Soup

1 medium onion, chopped

1 medium celery rib with
leaves, chopped

1 medium carrot, chopped

8 large cloves garlic, crushed

2 sprigs of parsley

1 bay leaf

¼ teaspoon dried thyme

½ teaspoon salt

¼ teaspoon peppercorns

1½ quarts water,
or more as needed

1 large waxy new potato, scrubbed,
and cut into ¾-inch cubes

Chopped fresh herbs, such as basil,
dill, or tarragon, for garnish

This vegetable soup is almost hearty, although one of its beauties is its light, but flavorful, simplicity. Some people cook the rice right in the soup, but I like to do it separately so you can have as much rice as you want. Some like their soup thickened with rice until it resembles porridge; others like just a sprinkle. By separately preparing a pot of grains, you can use whatever you prefer, from amaranth to wheat berries. Without rice, the soup can be strained to make a vegetable broth to use in other recipes. I recommend making a double batch, serving half as soup and straining the remainder for vegetable broth.

1. To make the vegetable soup, in a large pot, bring all of the ingredients except the potato to a boil over high heat, adding enough water to completely cover the vegetables. Reduce the heat to low and partially cover. Simmer very gently for 1 hour. Add the potato and cook until the stock is well flavored and the vegetables are tender, about 30 minutes.

2. Spoon rice into individual soup bowls and ladle the soup over the rice. Sprinkle with the herbs and serve immediately.

Makes 6 to 8 servings

Homemade Vegetable Broth

Pour the soup into a coarse wire sieve set over a large bowl. Discard the solids in the sieve. Cool the broth to room temperature then refrigerate or freeze in 2-cup containers. (The broth can be stored for up to 3 days covered and refrigerated, or frozen for up to 3 months.) Makes about 1½ quarts broth.

mixed venetian vegetable stew

Can Be Cooked in Under 30 Minutes

Boiled Rice (page 27), preferably made with Italian rice

1 tablespoon extra virgin olive oil

3 medium (1½ pounds) zucchini, well scrubbed and cut into ½-inch cubes

1 medium onion, chopped

1 medium celery rib with leaves, chopped

1 medium red bell pepper, seeded and chopped

1 large garlic clove, minced

2 cups frozen peas, rinsed under hot running water to separate

¼ teaspoon salt

¼ teaspoon freshly ground pepper

2 tablespoons all-purpose flour

1½ cups Homemade Vegetable Broth (page 126), vegetable bouillon, or canned broth

1 tablespoon chopped mint

½ cup freshly grated Parmesan cheese

Freshly grated Parmesan cheese, for serving

northern Italians love their risotto-like dish of rice and peas called *risi e bisi*. I've added a few more vegetables to make a colorful topping for boiled rice.

1. In a large dutch oven or flameproof casserole, heat the oil over medium heat. Add the zucchini, onion, celery, red pepper, and garlic. Cover and cook, stir-ring occasionally, until the vegetables begin to soften, about 6 minutes. Uncover and increase the heat to high. Cook until the vegetables are lightly browned, about 4 minutes. Add the peas, cover, and cook until tender, about 4 minutes. Season with the salt and pepper.

2. Sprinkle the vegetables with the flour and stir constantly for 1 minute. Stir in the broth and mint. Bring to a simmer. Reduce the heat to low and simmer until the sauce is thickened, about 2 minutes. Stir in the ½ cup grated Parmesan.

3. Spoon the rice into individual soup bowls and top with the vegetables. Serve immediately. Pass additional Parmesan cheese on the side.

Variations

Venetian Vegetable Stew with Fresh Peas: Use 2 cups fresh peas (from 2 pounds pods) instead of the frozen peas. Cook the peas in a saucepan of lightly salted boiling water over high heat until just tender, 3 to 5 minutes. Drain and rinse under cold water. Stir the cooked peas into the sauce after it has thickened. Cook until heated through, about 2 minutes.

Mixed Venetian Vegetable Stew with Pancetta: Before adding the vegetables in Step 1, cook 2 ounces (½ cup) chopped pancetta, prosciutto, or bacon in the oil until browned, about 5 minutes. Pour off all but 1 tablespoon of the oil in the pan. Instead of vegetable broth, use beef broth.

Makes 4 to 6 servings

roasted vegetables in orange teriyaki

Steamed Brown Rice (page 28),
  preferably made with short-grain rice

Orange Teriyaki

½ cup soy sauce

Grated zest of 1 orange

½ cup fresh orange juice

2 medium scallions, finely chopped

2 tablespoons mirin (see Note)
  or dry sherry

2 tablespoons Asian dark sesame oil

2 tablespoons minced fresh ginger

3 garlic cloves, minced

¼ teaspoon freshly ground
  black pepper

1 tablespoon light brown sugar,
  if not using mirin

1½ pounds broccoli, trimmed,
  stems cut crosswise into ¼-inch-
  thick slices, rest cut into florets

6 medium carrots (1 pound), cut into
  ¼-inch-thick rounds

1½ pounds portobello or large
  white button mushrooms, cut into
  ½-inch-thick slices

Sesame seeds, for garnish

roasting vegetables gives them depth of flavor and a crisp-tender crunch. Timing is the key. The most solid vegetables are roasted first, and the more delicate added later. Basted with an orange-based teriyaki marinade, the vegetables are especially good on hearty brown rice.

1. Position a rack in the top third of the oven and preheat to 550° F. Lightly oil a large (about 12 x 17-inch) roasting pan.

2. To make the teriyaki, in a medium bowl, whisk together the soy sauce, orange zest, orange juice, scallions, mirin or sherry, sesame oil, ginger, garlic, pepper, and brown sugar, if using sherry.

3. Place the broccoli stems and carrots in the roasting pan and toss with the teriyaki. Roast for 15 minutes, stirring occasionally. Remove from the oven, add the broccoli florets and mushrooms, and toss well to coat with the teriyaki. Return to the oven. Roast, stirring occasionally, until the broccoli is crisp-tender and lightly browned on the edges, about 15 minutes.

4. Spoon the rice into individual bowls, top with the vegetables and teriyaki, and sprinkle with the sesame seeds. Serve immediately.

Note: Mirin is a sweetened Japanese rice wine. The best quality is called hon mirin. It is available at Japanese markets, some supermarkets, and by mail order (see page 140).

Makes 4 to 6 servings

erna's make-in-your-sleep raspberry rice pudding

baked rum-raisin rice pudding

easy chocolate rice pudding with cherries

coconut rice pudding with tropical fruits

...dessert

I can't think of a better way to use leftover rice than making a luscious pudding. My only dilemma is what kind of pudding to make. Shall it be baked and served warm, or maybe folded into whipped cream and chilled?

Do I feel like an old-fashioned custardy pudding with raisins, or something more exotic with coconut or chocolate? This chapter offers four of my favorite rice puddings, each one in a distinctly different style.

Rice pudding is deliciously easy to make. Medium-grain rice, with its tender texture, makes the best rice pudding. These recipes all use leftover rice, as I believe rice pudding's appeal is its simplicity—you merely stir together a few ingredients and mix in a little leftover rice. But even something as simple as rice pudding has its little tricks to making it even better.

When rice is chilled, the starch in the grains hardens them into unappetizingly tough little bullets. If you like chilled rice pudding, be sure your rice is well cooked before using. I recommend recooking leftover rice for your pudding recipe in a little water for 10 minutes or so until it is quite soft (but not mushy). If necessary, drain the rice from its reheating water. I have very fond memories of my Grandmother Edith's chilled rice pudding, but when I first tried to reproduce it myself, the rice hardened into pellets. I was frustrated until I realized that my grandmother overcooked her rice, whereas I was using perfectly cooked rice that she would consider tough. When I made her pudding with recooked rice, it was just like the old days.

To encourage a smooth baked rice pudding, keep the temperature slow and even with a water bath. (In French cooking, this gentle cooking device is called a *bain-marie*, or Mary's bath, so named after the Virgin Mary, who is a symbol of temperate behavior.) The key to any custard is a temperature that doesn't rise above 325°F, as the eggs will curdle if cooked at a higher heat. The water bath acts as an insulator, not as a source of heat.

Here's the easiest way to set up a water bath without splashing water all over the kitchen. Preheat the oven. Open the oven and slide out the center oven rack a few inches. Place the rice pudding in its baking dish in a larger baking dish or roasting pan and put them on the oven rack. Pour enough hot water (from the tap, it doesn't have to be boiling) into the larger dish to come about halfway up the sides of the rice pudding dish. Gently slide the oven rack into the oven, being careful not to splash the water into the pudding. Don't overbake the pudding or it will curdle. It is done when a knife inserted 1 inch from the edge of the dish comes out clean. The center may still wobble a little when the dish is shaken, but it will continue to cook outside of the oven from the residual heat, and firm after cooling.

erna's make-in-your-sleep raspberry rice pudding

1½ cups cooked rice, preferably medium-grain

1½ cups heavy cream

¼ cup sugar

¾ teaspoon vanilla extract

⅓ cup seedless raspberry jam, stirred to loosen

½ pint fresh raspberries

My friend Erna Zahn is a born cook. This is how she makes her rice pudding, which she swears she can make in her sleep, it's so easy. Erna's family likes rice cooked until it's soft, so she is able to skip the recooking step. But if you like your rice cooked firm, recook the leftover rice until it is soft before making the pudding.

1. In a medium saucepan, bring ¼ cup water to a simmer over low heat. Add the cooked rice and cover. Simmer until the rice is very soft, about 10 minutes. Drain, if necessary, and cool completely.

2. In a chilled medium bowl, using a hand-held electric mixer set at high speed, beat the cream, sugar, and vanilla until stiff. Add the rice and raspberry preserves and fold until combined. Cover and chill for at least 1 hour.

3. Spoon into dessert bowls and sprinkle with the raspberries. Serve immediately.

Makes 4 to 6 servings

Left: **Baked Rum-Raisin Rice Pudding,** page 136.
Right: **Erna's Make-In-Your-Sleep Raspberry Rice Pudding,** this page.

baked rum-raisin rice pudding

Butter, for the baking dish

½ cup raisins

3 tablespoons dark rum

1 cup cooked rice, preferably medium-grain

4 large eggs

½ cup sugar

1 teaspoon vanilla extract

2 cups milk

Ground cinnamon, for sprinkling

this is my grandmother's rice pudding, in all its simple glory, although the rum is my touch.

1. Position a rack in the center of the oven and preheat to 325° F. Lightly butter an 8-inch square glass baking dish.

2. In a small bowl, combine the raisins and rum. Let stand, stirring occasionally, until the raisins are plumped, about 1 hour, or place in a microwave-safe bowl, cover with plastic wrap, and microwave on High (100%) for 1 minute. Let stand for 5 minutes.

3. In a medium saucepan, bring ⅓ cup water to a simmer over low heat. Add the cooked rice and cover. Simmer until the rice is quite soft, about 10 minutes. Drain, if necessary.

4. In a medium bowl, whisk the eggs, sugar, and vanilla. Gradually whisk in the milk until well blended. Stir in the raisins with their soaking liquid and the rice. Pour into the prepared dish.

5. Place the dish in a larger baking pan. Place in the oven and pour in enough hot water to come halfway up the sides of the dish. Bake until a knife inserted about 1 inch from the edge of the custard comes out clean, but the center still seems wobbly, about 45 minutes. Remove from the water bath and cool slightly. Sprinkle the top lightly with cinnamon. Serve warm, at room temperature, or chilled.

Makes 4 to 6 servings

easy chocolate rice pudding with cherries

¼ cup dried cherries

2 tablespoons kirsch or other cherry-flavored liqueur, or hot water

¼ cup sugar

1 tablespoon cornstarch

2 cups milk, heated to scalding

1 cup cooked long-grain rice

3 ounces high-quality imported bittersweet chocolate, finely chopped

1 teaspoon vanilla extract

Sweetened whipped cream (optional)

This is my friend Marie Simmons's recipe for one of the best, and most simple, rice puddings around. Her chocolate embellishment takes a good thing and makes it even better, and I gild the lily with kirsch-soaked dried cherries. (If you are serving this to kids, soak the cherries in hot water instead of liqueur.) Because this pudding is served warm, you don't have to worry about the rice's getting hard, a consideration with most chilled rice puddings.

1. In a small bowl, soak the cherries in the liqueur, stirring often, until plumped, about 1 hour. (Or microwave the cherries, uncovered, for 45 seconds on high power. Stir, and let sit for 5 minutes.)

2. In a heavy-bottomed medium saucepan, combine the sugar and cornstarch. Gradually whisk in the hot milk to dissolve the cornstarch. Stir in the rice, chocolate, and plumped cherries with their liquid. Cook over medium heat, stirring constantly, until the mixture thickens and the chocolate melts, about 5 minutes. Remove from the heat and stir in the vanilla.

3. Ladle the pudding into 4 custard cups. Cover each with plastic wrap pressed directly onto the surface of the pudding. Pierce the plastic a few times with the tip of a sharp knife to allow the steam to escape. Cool, and serve at room temperature. If desired, top each serving with a dollop of whipped cream.

Makes 4 servings

coconut rice pudding with tropical fruits

2 cups cooked medium-grain rice

3 cups canned unsweetened coconut
milk (see page 54)

¾ cup plus 2 tablespoons
(packed) light brown sugar

4 large egg yolks

2 tablespoons cornstarch

1 teaspoon vanilla extract

2 cups chopped ripe fruits, such
as mango, papaya, banana, and
raspberries, in any combination

Sweetened whipped cream,
for garnish

Coconut milk turns many desserts into extra-special treats, and this sinfully rich stovetop rice pudding is no exception.

1. In a heavy-bottomed, medium saucepan, bring the rice and coconut milk to a simmer over medium heat. Reduce the heat to low and cook, stirring often, until the rice is very soft, about 10 minutes. Stir in the brown sugar until dissolved.

2. In a medium bowl, whisk the egg yolks and cornstarch. Gradually whisk in about ½ cup of the hot rice mixture. Pour into the saucepan and cook, stirring constantly, until it comes to a simmer, then stir for 1 minute. Stir in the vanilla. Transfer to a medium bowl. Press a piece of plastic wrap directly onto the surface of the pudding. Using a small sharp knife, poke a few holes to act as vents in the plastic wrap. Cool the pudding to room temperature. Refrigerate until chilled, at least 4 hours or overnight.

3. Spoon the rice pudding into large wine glasses, layering with the fruit. Top with a dollop of whipped cream and serve immediately.

Variation

Gingered Coconut Rice Pudding: Stir ½ cup finely chopped crystallized ginger into the pudding with the vanilla. Garnish each serving with additional chopped crystallized ginger.

Makes 6 to 8 servings

Left: **Easy Chocolate Rice Pudding with Cherries,**
page 137.
Right: **Coconut Rice Pudding with Tropical Fruits,**
this page.

mail-order sources

Dean and Deluca
560 Broadway, New York, NY 10012
1-800-221-7714 or 1-212-431-1691
Domestic and imported rice,
dried chilies, tomatillos

Gibbs Wild Rice
10400 Billings Road, Live Oak, CA 95953
1-800-824-4932
Cultivated wild rice

Louisiana Rice Company
Route 3, Box 55, Welsh, LA 70591
1-318-734-2251
Louisiana popcorn rice

Lundberg Family Farms
Box 369, Richvale, CA 95974-0369
1-916-882-4551
Aromatic domestic rice, mixed rice blends

Northern Lakes Wild Rice
P.O. Box 592, Teton Village, WY 83025
1-307-733-7192 or 1-218-654-5851
(September and October)
Hand-harvested wild rice

The Oriental Pantry
423 Great Road, Acton, MA 01720
1-800-828-0368
Domestic and imported rice, Thai yellow
curry paste, fish sauce, dried lemon grass,
coconut milk, mirin

Walnut Acres
Penns Creek, PA 17862
1-800-433-3998
Organic white, brown, and wild rice, mixed
rice blends, electric rice cookers

index

table of equivalents

The exact equivalents in these tables have been rounded for convenience.

Rices

Arborio rice	1 cup	200 g	7 oz
Asian-style rice	1 cup	195 g	6¾ oz
Basmati rice	1 cup	195 g	6¾ oz
Black rice:			
long grain	1 cup	195 g	6¾ oz
short grain	1 cup	220 g	7½ oz
Brown rice:			
long grain	1 cup	195 g	6¾ oz
medium grain	1 cup	200 g	7 oz
short grain	1 cup	220 g	7½ oz
Jasmine rice	1 cup	195 g	6¾ oz
Red rice	1 cup	220 g	7½ oz
Spanish rice			
(Valencia rice)	1 cup	200 g	7 oz
White rice:			
long grain	1 cup	195 g	6¾ oz
medium grain	1 cup	200 g	7 oz
short grain	1 cup	220 g	7½ oz
Wild rice	1 cup	185 g	6½ oz

Other Grains

Amaranth	1 cup	195 g	6¾ oz
Barley (pearled)	1 cup	205 g	7¼ oz
Bulgur (medium)	1 cup	160 g	5½ oz
Corn grits (Polenta)	1 cup	160 g	5½ oz
Couscous	1 cup	175 g	6 oz
Kamut	1 cup	190 g	6¾ oz
Kasha	1 cup	180 g	6½ oz
Millet	1 cup	200 g	7 oz
Polenta (Corn grits)	1 cup	160 g	5½ oz
Quinoa	1 cup	180 g	6½ oz
Rye berries	1 cup	195 g	6¾ oz
Spelt	1 cup	195 g	6¾ oz
Triticale	1 cup	195 g	6¾ oz
Wheat berries	1 cup	195 g	6¾ oz

US/UK	Metric
oz=ounce	g=gram
lb=pound	kg=kilogram
in=inch	mm=millimeter
ft=foot	cm=centimeter
tbl=tablespoon	ml=milliliter
fl oz=fluid ounce	l=liter
qt=quart	

Weights

US/UK	Metric
1 oz	30 g
2 oz	60 g
3 oz	90 g
4 oz (¼ lb)	125 g
5 oz (⅓ lb)	155 g
6 oz	185 g
7 oz	220 g
8 oz (½ lb)	250 g
10 oz	315 g
12 oz (¾ lb)	375 g
14 oz	440 g
16 oz (1 lb)	500 g

Length Measures

US/UK	Metric
⅛ in	3 mm
¼ in	6 mm
½ in	12 mm
1 in	2.5 cm
2 in	5 cm
3 in	7.5 cm
4 in	10 cm
12 in/1 ft	30 cm

Oven Temperatures

Fahrenheit	Celsius	Gas
250	120	½
275	140	1
300	150	2
325	160	3
350	180	4
375	190	5
400	200	6
425	220	7
450	230	8
475	240	9
500	260	10

Liquids

US	Metric	UK
2 tbl	30 ml	1 fl oz
¼ cup	60 ml	2 fl oz
⅓ cup	80 ml	3 fl oz
½ cup	125 ml	4 fl oz
⅔ cup	160 ml	5 fl oz
¾ cup	180 ml	6 fl oz
1 cup	250 ml	8 fl oz
1½ cups	375 ml	12 fl oz
2 cups	500 ml	16 fl oz
4 cups/1 qt	1 l	32 fl oz